Library of
Davidson College

IN THE TROJAN DITCH

also by C. H. Sisson

AN ASIATIC ROMANCE
CHRISTOPHER HOMM

THE SPIRIT OF BRITISH ADMINISTRATION
WALTER BAGEHOT

ART AND ACTION
ENGLISH POETRY 1900–1950

VERSIONS AND PERVERSIONS OF HEINE
CATULLUS

THE LONDON ZOO
NUMBERS
METAMORPHOSES

C. H. Sisson

IN THE TROJAN DITCH

Collected Poems
& Selected Translations

DUFOUR EDITIONS, INC.

NOTE
Part I contains most of the poems from *The London Zoo* (Abelard-Schuman, 1961), *Numbers* and *Metamorphoses* (Methuen, 1965 and 1968) and more than enough new matter to have made another volume of the same kind. The recent poems come first and the earliest last. Hitherto unpublished earlier poems have been put more or less in their chronological places.
Part II consists of translations selected from *Versions and Perversions of Heine* (Gaberbocchus, 1955) and *Catullus* (MacGibbon & Kee, 1966), together with unpublished work including the whole of a version of Vergil's Eclogues.

Acknowledgements are due to Grossman Publishers, New York, for permission to reprint matter from *Catullus*, and to the editors of *The New English Weekly, Botteghe Oscure, Other Voices, Arena, Holy Door, The Scotsman, Die Neue Zürcher Zeitung, X, Agenda, Ishmael, The Dublin Magazine, Aquarius, Two Rivers, Anthos, Caret, New Fire, Critical Quarterly,* and *Poetry Nation,* in which matter from one or other parts of the book has appeared.

ISBN 0 8023 1263 2
LC 75- 15245
All rights reserved

© C. H. Sisson 1975

No part of this publication may be reproduced, stored in a retrieval system, or transmitted in any form or by any means – except by a reviewer who wishes to quote brief passages for inclusion in a magazine, newspaper, or broadcast – without prior permission in writing from the publisher.

First published in the United States
of America 1975
by Dufour Editions, Inc.,
Chester Springs, Pennsylvania 19425

Printed in Great Britain
by Unwin Brothers Limited
The Gresham Press, Old Woking, Surrey
A member of the Staples Printing Group

CONTENTS

PART I – COLLECTED POEMS

13 FOREWORD
14 Martigues
17 In Arles
18 Dialogue of the Soul and God
21 In Insula Avalonia
27 Ha! Vieillesse
28 Somerton Moor
29 Sumptuary Laws
29 In Spring-Time
30 In the Great World
30 Morpheus
31 Seeming
32 Mortalia
32 Saint Anthony
33 The Usk
35 Good Friday
36 Summer Green
36 Envy
37 Aller Church
37 Van Dieman's Land
39 In the Trojan Ditch
     I. *Troilus and Cressida*
     II. *Helen*
     III. *Athene*
41 Ambition
41 Ovid in Pontus
42 Daphne
42 Trafalgar Square
43 The Crucifix
43 Pickers and Stealers
44 The Salad
44 Evening
45 The Discarnation
62 Hactenus Arvorum Cultus
62 Palaestra and Ampelisca
63 Anacreon
63 Hod Hill

63 No Address
64 For Patrick Swift
64 Human Relations
65 Virgini Senescens
68 Eurydice
69 The Rope
70 The Garden Of Epicurus
70 The Person
71 Every Reality is a Kind of Sign
71 The Recollection
73 The Alley-Way
74 The Withdrawal
74 The Spectre
79 The Regrets
80 The Cave
81 The Shape
81 On the Coast
82 The Queen of Lydia
84 The Adventurer
84 The Affirmative
85 On my Fifty-First Birthday
85 In Brewer Street
86 Horatius
87 Adam
88 Homo Sapiens is of No Importance
89 The Man with a Family
89 Orpheus
90 Metamorphoses
98 Stanza
99 An Essay on God and Man
100 The Consequence
102 Catullus
103 In Preparation for an Epitaph
103 Words
103 My Life and Times
106 The Nature of Man
106 A Letter to John Donne
107 A and B
109 Good-Day, Citizen
109 At First
110 Eros
110 Act Munday

111 An Old Man
112 The Thrush
112 Adam and Eve
113 Easter
113 Nuptials
114 By the Lift Gate
114 Great Down
115 A Young Woman
116 Grandmother
116 Loquitur Senex
117 Things Seen
118 The Nature-Lover
118 The Lion Man
118 The Temple
119 In Memoriam Cecil de Vall
120 Eclogue
124 No Title
125 Thomas de Quincey
125 The Theology of Fitness
126 What a Piece of Work is Man
128 A Girl
129 The Reckoning
129 From a Train
130 Amour Propre
131 Consequences
131 Numbers
133 The Shortest Day
133 Christmas at the Greyhound
134 The Luxembourg
134 The Leopard and the Lynx
135 Two Shepherds
135 The Ragman
136 The Un-red Deer
136 The Deer-Park
137 Heroes
138 Ellick Farm
138 Money
139 Knole
139 Cranmer
140 Tintagel
140 At an International Conference
141 Nude Studies

141 The Art of Living
142 Ide Hill
142 In Honour of J. H. Fabre
143 Commuters
143 Victoria Station
144 Family Fortunes
145 Ightham Woods
145 The Origin of Species
146 In Autumn
146 At the Airport
147 The Conversation of Age
147 St Gennys
147 On the Way Home
148 Maurras, Young and Old
149 Vienna
150 The Night Ferry
150 A Monument in Milan
150 A Duckling
151 In Kent
151 Sparrows Seen from an Office
152 Fellfoot
152 On a Civil Servant
152 In a Dark Wood
153 La Biologie
153 Moriturus
154 Epictetus
154 The Body in Asia
156 In the Hills
156 On a Troopship

PART II – SELECTED TRANSLATIONS

159 FOREWORD

    Heine
163   *In October 1849: Gelegt hat sich der starke Wind*
164   *Es gibt zwei Sorten Ratten*
166   *Die Briten zeigten sich sehr rüde*
167   *Der Nachtwind durch die Luken pfeift*
168   *Deutschland, Canto II: Während die Kleine von Himmelslust*
    Anon. 12th-13th Century
170   *Por quoi me bat mes maris?*

	Catullus
171	Selected Poems
	Ovid
181	From Book I of the *Metamorphoses*
	Propertius
188	In Allusion to Propertius, I, iii
	Vergil
189	Palinurus (*Aeneid* V, 835ff)
189	The Descent (from *Aeneid* VI)
193	The Eclogues
	Horace
221	*Carmen Saeculare*
223	*Iam satis terris nivis atque dirae* (I, ii)
224	*Tu ne quaesieris, scire nefas, quem mihi, quem tibi* (I, xi)
225	*Quid dedicatum poscit Apollinem* (I, xxxi)
225	*Rectius vives, Licini, neque altum* (II, x)
226	*Iam pauca aratro iugera regiae* (II, xv)
227	*Eheu fugaces, Postume, Postume* (II, xiv)

Part I: Collected Poems

Foreword

THE EARLIEST POEM here reprinted (on p. 156) was written on a troopship going south through tropical waters. It is not altogether the work of an innocent beginner: I was nearly thirty. More poems were written in military camps in Bengal and the late North-West Frontier Province (pp. 154–6). There was a gap of several years, then the break to the surface which occurred with the poems entitled 'Fellfoot' and 'In a Dark Wood' (p. 152).

That much of history explains how the bulk of the volume is the work of a man going onwards from thirty-five – poems of the return journey, therefore. My beginnings were altogether without facility, and when I was forced into verse it was through having something not altogether easy to say.

In a manner this defines the nature of the poet's problem. There is no question, as it has come to me, of filling note-books with what one knows already. Indeed as the inevitable facility comes, the conscious task becomes the rejection of whatever appears with the face of familiarity. The writing of poetry is, in a sense, the opposite of writing what one wants to write, and it is because of the embarrassing growth of the area of consciousness which writing, as indeed the other serious encounters of life, produces that one has recourse to the conscious manipulation of translation, as it were to distract one while the unwanted impulses free themselves under the provocation of another's thought. I have come in the end to have great sympathy with Dryden, who having pushed his way this way and that at the end of his days took pride in being able to do a translation better than any of them. He was glad, I imagine, to be able to release the energies of poetry without passing for having said anything of his own. I do not pretend that my path has led me so far. There are other enabling distractions – reasoning and analysis, mythology and other narrative, properly used. All these are really modes of the problem of form.

The claim of a collection like this is in the continuity of statement which underlies the historical recording, analysis or imitation and is recognisable in the development of rhythm rather than in overt logical connections. The proof of the poem – any poem – is in its rhythm and that is why critical determination has in the end to await that unarguable perception.

Martigues

I.

Myrtle, roses and thyme
And the rose laurel:
I too have something that I wish to forget
There, where the woodland path
Passes into the concrete
And my tears are for a master.
At the gate I picked a leaf of laurel and said:
Dante
Wore these pointed leaves.
Here, in the bitter south,
A madman, between gaolers.
Whisper it to the myrtles we may, crushing the past
In our tingling fingers,
Or picking the thyme.
But the rose laurel

It is all I have, the bitten past,
Not all I came to.
Speeches were made and names taken, the heart
Burst out of his side.
No love like the unspoken
Ferocity, and bitter tears, a battle
Standing instead with brimming eyes
Looking out over the *étang*
The poverty of a few fish
And a garden of roses.

I too have something that I wish to forget.
Myrtle and roses, the same.
Controversy among apes is no custom
And my limbs fell hard
Against the rail of the scuttled ship. You may cup your eye-balls
For ordinary uses now.
My faith
Sprang into the air with indignation.

II.

At the corner of the streets
The fishermen stand in groups
With brown faces: they have them from the Moors
And the wind blowing across the *étang*.

In the garden,
Pierre, or perhaps Adam.
I shake him by the hand, brown also,
A fisherman's face, gardener's rather.
Help us with the language of saints.
Adam spoke
Softly, and in the old *patois,*
Knowing no other.
Myrtle, roses and thyme
And the rose laurel
Never to be let go.
I took him by the hand
Old friend
Whom I have never seen
Your ghost is my beginning, I have tears
For what is here forgotten
And in the winter of my age my hand
Cut the air with scimitars.

III.

Roses and thyme
But leave the myrtle, leave the myrtle here
Roses and thyme
Fed on a garden where I made my home
And southward facing over the *étang*.
In Somerset I crumble up the soil
And linger on a terrace looking south
So minds have ears no voices
They have eyes
Which look upon the land and do no harm
But avarice is cupid in this game.
Yet love came after all, olive and rush,
The tart wine held under the cupping hand.

One taste of death. Good-night to all this lake.
The olives in the garden after all
Eat up the man and put him under ground
How should he turn his hand?

IV.

Pallas Athene, wisdom in all this,
Mistress of olives and the curling prow
Let not your lids drop on this falling earth.
Set enmities at rest or let there be
Sufficient enmity to stir up love
And bring the sword before you bring smooth tongues,
Harsh enmities are best
And Judas put his silver in the ground.

V.

Night falls, perhaps, upon my wide *étang*,
Joseph of Arimethea riding home.
The Saintes Maries
Await another pilgrim at this time
But now must sleep. And did he sleep or wake
Who walked upon this terrace in his dream?
The Saintes Maries put out their lights at last
And Joseph's ship touches a barren stone.

VI.

He took a flower
And gave it in a morning without hope.
Hand down the rose
Hand down the myrtle, stuff the air with thyme.
There in a garden where it all began
Seek nothing for yourself. Seek nothing more
Than time will offer to dishonesty
And patience and the like. Silence at last
And Abraham's voice seeps through the air.
David is King. And then the dragons come
The thud of horses over the Camargue,
But silence first. The rose,
Myrtle crushed in the hand
And the rose laurel.

In Arles

The bitterness is covered but not buried
A little light earth, that is all
The centuries will not discover, nor the footfall
Be light upon me.

Lying there, in the light, unable to speak
No penny upon my lips
To send me thither to the Tartarus of Time.
Have mercy, Lord.

My eyes open, with eyelids pulled apart
I stand here before time
Have mercy goddesses, standing in the long avenues.
Death is in your keeping.

The bright eye, let me never be parted from it
I hear the drum now
I hear the whistle, there are pipes in this shrubbery
And the owl is near.

Pallas Athene, my dear
Look kindly upon my plain endeavours.
Light spins over the Camargue.
Evening is here.

Christ of the mass-priests, farewell, yet in the shadows
These have my tears
A crucifixion, a crucifixion, and the dogs howl
Nearer than death.

My tears, and my Saviour, this stone
The candle to light upon him
Eyes in the dark, the hidden light
And Pallas Athene is gone.

Yet she stands there at the entrance, smiling
The horses thunder by
– Is that money with which I cross her palm? –
I will come directly.

Dialogue of the Soul and God, or of Psyche with Cupid

1.

Love, hear me come
I rustle up the stairs and am with God
Come over me
You winged ecstatic stranger in my bed

I come
Psyche lie in the dawn
And do not turn your head
I may be Christ

I lie
Covered in flowers
Nature's fair canopy, and dream
So must it be

I wing
Across an azure main, far out
The sea is mine
White gulls

Though I lie still, I fly
With you, against the cloud
It cannot be
Yet I am you I know

Ah, take no candle dear
To spoil your dream
I am the edge of things
And will be gone

Will you not love
The resting limbs in bed?
Not I, my dear, the wind
The kami-kaze I.

II.

Lord Wind
I am your patience so I am not I

If you were you
I would dissolve
So not in peace

I, I
The entropy of every beast
Sigh out your wind

Dissolve
Be less than nothing now
I hawk

You kestrel on the wing
What wind
Can hold you now?

My police
Is in my eye

My current flows away
Less than the wind

Hawk not

Not I

Descending

I

I rise upon the wind

I, I?

III.

No mind has spoken yet

Nor will
You catch-cheat, catch-care face
You foot

I foot
Wandering upon the ground

You badger-track, you walk

Split eye
Half looking up, half down
What shall I do?

Do nothing more, but sleep
Geschwind

IV.

This is the end
Of all I ever made

You make?
The makeless maker is the make of you

Down eyes

Down head
And do you feel my foot across the nape?

My hair
Mops up your feet as Mary Magdalen's did

Slut, I am there.

In Insula Avalonia

I.

Huge bodies driven on the shore by sleep
The mountain-woman rocks might fall upon
And in the cavity the heaped-up man.

Sleep on the island like a witty zone
Seas break about it, frolicking like youth
But in the mists are eyes, not dancers, found.

Hurt is the shepherd on the inland hill
He has a cot, a staff and certain sheep
Stones are his bed, his tables and his bread.

This is not where the sirens were, I think
But somewhere, over there, the next approach
Behind that other island in the mist.

That was the song, beyond the linnet-call
At the cliff's edge, below the plunging gull
The fish it found, the enemy or Christ.

II.

Counting up all the ways I have been a fool,
In the long night, although the convent clock
Winds several hours around Medusa's locks,

Geryon and Chrysaor are with me now
– Sure there was bad blood in that family –
And yet the worst of all was done by love.

The fool: but not the bow and naked babe
But top-coat murderers with sullen looks
And yet Medusa was a temple harlot.

Under the river-bank a seeping wind
Ripples the bubbles from a passing fish
No colder memory than gloomy Dis.

Look, for you must, upon the fine appearance,
The creature had it and is formless dead.
Now come no nearer than to straws in glass.

III.

Dark wind, dark wind that makes the river black
– Two swans upon it are the serpent's eyes –
Wind through the meadows as you twist your heart.

Twisted are trees, especially this oak
Which stands with all its leaves throughout the year;
There is no Autumn for its golden boughs

But Winter always and the lowering sky
That hangs its blanket lower than the earth
Which we are under in this Advent-tide.

Not even ghosts. The banks are desolate
With shallow snow between the matted grass
Home of the dead but there is no one here.

What is a church-bell in this empty time?
The geese come honking in a careless skein
Sliding between the mort plain and the sky.

What augury? Or is there any such?
They pass over the oak and leave me there
Not even choosing, by the serpent's head.

IV.

O there are summer-riders
On the plain
          in file or two by two

It is a dream

For Winter, one by one, is wringing us
The withers, one, and scrotum-tight the other

Yet I am here
Looking down on the plain, my elbow on
The sill

From which I night by night and day by day
Watch
       for the moon pours swimmingly

Upon this field, this stream
That feeds my sleep.

Be night
Be young
The morning half begun
Palls on the waiting mind and makes it scream

O Minnich, Minnich

Who is the lady there by Arthur's lake?
None is. A willow and a tuft of grass
But over bones it broods, as over mine
Somewhere
Except
       nowhere

Bind up your temples and begone from here
No need to answer. What is there to fear?
Only the winds that soughs, and soughs, and soughs.
Some say it does, and others contradict
Some say sleep strengthens, others that it kills
This music comes
               from Wendover I think
Where meaning is at least, there, sure, am I.

v.

Out in the sunlight there I am afraid
For dark depends upon the nascent mind
The light, the envy and the world at large

A field for flood, and fish and such-like deer
The willows standing in between the pools
Great siege this morning, in the morning-time

The water rustles like a turning page
Write then who will, but write upon the stream
Which passes nonchalantly through the hedge

No word of mine will ever reach the sea
For mine and words are clean contrary things
Stop here for envy, go there for your love

For love of persons are the passing geese
Swans on the flood, the dopping water-fowl
The cloud that cumbers while the sky is blue.

Awful at nights, the mind is blue today
Enlarged without a purpose like a lake
For purpose pricks the bubble of our thoughts.

Climb back to sleep, the savage in that mine
Picks with his teeth and leaves his skull to dry
O skull and cross-bones on the earthen floor

My earth, my water, my redundant trees
Breaking the surface like a stitch in skin.
No word but weather, let me be like that.

VI.

A ruminant in darkness. So am I
Between the skin and half a hope of hell
Tell me till morning where the savage stops.

His eyes beside the fire. The burning peat
Is quiet, quiet, quiet till it shrieks
Not what the hammer was but what it says

The eyes on Thursday and the mind that waits
For sabbaths of intent but does no thing
Not seeking, waiting for a peaceful end

What wind is in the trees? What water laps
Extravagantly round the seeping hedge?
A house on sticks, where several yearned before

The skin, the furze, the movement into sleep
The watery lids beside the river bank
Mirrors of emptiness, O what way in?

VII.

A mine of mind, descend who can that way
As down a staircase to the inner ring
Where figures are at liberty, and play

A plain of ghosts, among the rest a girl
(And none had touched her, though the serpent's teeth
Met in her heel below the flying skirt)

She gathered flowers, exacting from their grace
An outward parallel for grace of skin,
Petals for fingers, petals for arms and legs.

This transient surface is the thing I seek
No more, perhaps, than scale upon the eyes
Do not walk with her, winds are blown that way

A storm of leaves and all may disappear
And yet below the circle of my mind
Playing in spring-time there is Proserpine.

But I am rather Cerberus than Dis
Neither receive nor yet pursue this child
Nor am I Orpheus who could bring her back.

I stand and roar and only shake my chain
The river passes and gives others sleep
I am the jaws nothing will pass between.

VIII.

The mind beyond the reach of human time
Mine or another's, let me now perceive
Time has turned sour upon the earth for me

A little earth, walking upon the earth
A molehill, Mother, on your credent slopes
But moving, time against me, everywhere

This is the lump out of which I was made
The hands, the feet, the brain no less is mud
What does not crumble must remain in shape

The shape of man, but moles are better off
Boring the hill-side like a nit in cheese
They asked for blindness, that is what they have

But I for light, for sleep, for anything
Moving my hands across the surfaced world
Exacerbate in darkness, though alive

I never came from any natural thing
To take this shape which is not mine at all
Yet I am I am I and nothing more

If any took this shape I took this shape
Yet taking what I did not ask to have
And being nothing till I took this shape

The shape of shafts of light and falling suns
Meteors incarcerate in balls of mud
A cracked example of a better kind

Admit you came because you could not know
Walk in the garden as you did one day
And if you cannot flatter, answer back.

IX.

Some seek examples in the world of sense
They slide across the retina like dreams
Yet are objective in the world of deeps

Which swimmers may attempt, that move all ways
Across the current, from the pebbly floor
Up to the surface where the morning breaks

If any capture what the water-weed
Holds brightly like a bubble on its stem
Or what may disappear in lengthening dark

Volumes of sleep will turn the swimmer's arm
His leg will gently bump the feathered rock
Gulls cry above, sleep has no place for them

A call, a cry, a murder in the street
Is sign of others lonely as yourself
The Lord have mercy, others may as well.

x.

I do not know and cannot know indeed
And do not want a word to tell me so
A sentence is construction more than I.

I feel, I vomit. I am left to earth
To trample and be trampled, in my turn
But always rotting from the day I came

Thy kingdom come. And could I pray indeed
I would be höhnisch and destroy the world
This is not what is meant and nor am I.

So let my silence fasten on a rock
Be lichen, that is plenty, for my mind
And not be where I was. Where is he? Gone

The empty space is better than himself
But best of all when, certain winters past,
No one says: There he was, I knew him well.

Ha! Vieillesse

Good-bye then, love, good-bye holiness
In which at one time I put my trust
One of you disappointed me and one I could not attain
I begin to hobble as I grow old.

Somerton Moor

I.

You are unusual, but the touch
Of innocence may sear a mind.
I know who say so, for I am
The prisoner of a loving ghost

O death, come quickly, for the fiend
Crosses the marshes with my tears.

II.

Under the peat, dark mystery of earth,
Fire of the hearth, enchanter of my heart
The smoke that rises is a sacrifice
The peat moves over in its sodden sleep

And I, who should have touched her with my wand
Let her evade beneath the burning turf
And now through smoke and bitterness I speak
Words she would recognise and no one else
And she can no more hear than oyster-ears.

III.

Last speech. Accustomed as I am to speech
And she to silence, excellence is hard
For nothing that is facile can be heard
And nothing hard can be endured for long.
So sleep. Pass out between the willow-boughs
Out of my dream into the cool of death.
There, where the resurrection that you hope,
Though tardy, comes at last
The instrument I carry is untuned.

Sumptuary Laws

Still with the hope of being understood,
Of understanding myself
Or understanding someone else,
I engaged in restless action.
It was no good.
First because
It had no issue, secondly because
If it could have had, I would no longer care.
The problems of age are semblant, one thing
Like another, no thing identical,
The things having been seen, the passions
Expended in better times by a better man.
So outwardly and above
We turn, gracious and empty
The old hypocrites, counting the stars,
Loving the children, counting them like money.
Thanking what stars we have that the wrong turnings
Have all been taken, a life of comfort
Assured, as it may be, to the last deception
I could call this life respectable but
I must call it mine, which is worse.

In Spring-Time

Another time, this way the primrose,
I lost my way before my age was full
In a deep valley. And the cleft said nothing
But perhaps, I am limestone, grey
Lichen upon me, grey.

No voice. Came summer yet no voice. Came once
The lark, the plover and the hare in March.
Almost the wind is speech.

What turns I took and then the cock-crow came
Not once but many times.

In the Great World

In the great world where beauty is
A rarity, ambition is
As common as the dust we eat.
And who, I ask myself, are you?
You are the child against the wall
The fierce nun's ruler did not hit.
You are the younger sister, strong
Because the house took care of you.
You are the virgin with a smile
And beauty as your best excuse,
The tatty girl protected by
The aura of the well-to-do;
The office wonder who performed
The gagne-pain of a city lout –
What is so wonderful in this?
The mind is what the eye can see;
The only freedom is to give.

Morpheus

Naked people
Stepping, under mackintoshes
Through the dim city

The elect, the dead
The indifferent, head on
Into the underground. Morpheus.

What underneath? Proserpine dances
Exactly with legs, arms curled
About her head like a duster

There are green fields, below
Memory cannot reach, trees discover
Or old tales render probable.

It was a snake, some say
Bit at her ankle. So
I would myself.

It was a thorn
Entangled her. I
Could wind about her.

It was the wind
Caught and advanced her flying
Hair. It was tears distresses

Of my hope and finding
Destroyed, unkindly, what hope there was.
That was my failure.

So against the crowd, perfect
I stand like a lamp-post, they flow past me
Stoney eyes, mine or theirs.

Seeming

What the imagination could only imagine
Is, ah how different from the thing done
Which is only a done thing, fine
To the spectator perhaps, but not to me.

It is somebody else's imagination.
Beauty, are you so?
My heart craves for you. Eaten out, hollow
What is this space for then, and how lived in?

Hollow heart also, you have nothing to live for.
It could not be me, for I am nothing at all.
Are you there, certainty, behind that beauty?
Are you there, or what?

Mortalia

In the leisurely days which precede my death
There is nothing I shall not regret. Dorset my hills
You have the shapes I have missed, the smile
Of contentment that was never mine.
Nothing but tears is hidden under your soil.

Saint Anthony

There were no chances and changes about a life
That was, after all, given over to resisting devils.
There were no events after that but
Many imaginary temptations.
A happy life this: beneficent, for
He protected sage martyrs against himself
Fly-blown and fly-proof, a concentration of follies
– Who had started with twenty years in remote Egypt
Of suave girls, silk wrappings, and fast cars.

The Usk

Christ is the language which we speak to God
And also God, so that we speak in truth;
He in us, we in him, speaking
To one another, to him, the City of God.

I.
Such a fool as I am you had better ignore
Tongue twist, malevolent, fat mouthed
I have no language but that other one
His the Devil's, no mouse I, creeping out of the cheese
With a peaked cap scanning the distance
Looking for truth.
Words when I have them, come out, the Devil
Encouraging, grinning from the other side of the street
And my tears
Streaming, a blubbered face, when I am not laughing
Where in all this
Is calm, measure,
Exactness
The Lord's peace?

II.
Nothing is in my own voice because I have not
Any. Nothing in my own name
Here inscribed on water, nothing but flow
A ripple, outwards. Standing beside the Usk
You flow like truth, river, I will get in
Over me, through me perhaps, river let me be crystalline
As I shall not be, shivering upon the bank.
A swan passed. So is it, the surface, sometimes
Benign like a mirror, but not I passing, the bird.

III.
Under the bridge, meet reward, the water
Falling in cascades or worse, you devil, for truthfulness
Is no part of the illusion, the clear sky
Is not yours, the water
Falling not yours

Only the sheep
Munching at the river brim
Perhaps

IV.
What I had hoped for, the clear line
Tremulous like water but
Clear also to the stones underneath
Has not come that way, for my truth
Was not public enough, nor perhaps true.
Holy Father, Almighty God
Stop me before I speak

        – *per Christum.*

V.
Lies on my tongue. Get up and bolt the door
For I am coming not to be believed
The messenger of anything I say.
So I am come, stand in the cold tonight
The servant of the grain upon my tongue,
Beware, I am the man, and let me in.

VI.
So speech is treasured, for the things it gives
Which I can not have, for I speak too plain
Yet not so plain as to be understood
It is confusion and a madman's tongue.
Where drops the reason, there is no one by.
Torture my mind: and so swim through the night
As envy cannot touch you, or myself
Sleep comes, and let her, warm at my side, like death.
The Holy Spirit and the Holy One
Of Israel be my guide. So among tombs
Truth may be sought, and found, if we rejoice
With Ham and Shem and Japhet in the dark
The ark rolls onward over a wide sea.
Come sleep, come lightning, comes the dove at last.

Good Friday

Christ, on Good Friday,
   I sit and mope.
      Hope
Is out of place, today.
Penance is not my way.

I, who hope little,
   Contrairy, find
      Mind
Today say that it will
Rather than sit still,

Rather than hear thud
   The bumping cross,
      Loss
Echo here, garden mud
Turn up here as blood.

Teach me to repent.
   I will not, I.
      Die
I will, for easement
Only, my will is bent.

Make straight my will, it
   May be if not
      Rotting
In me as mine, fit
Matter for a vain wit.

Nothing is mine, let
   Me know this now.
      How,
Why and what, are set
Like dishes before me, not to eat yet.

Summer Green

The voluntary world is far from me
Therefore I came here, where the woods fall down
Pell-mell into the fields. The timber lies
Broken and does not care, the spread leaves hold
Like fingers, air and let it run away.

Envy

Be prudent, comrade, as the wind
Which does not let itself be seen.
   My spleen
Exacerbates your skill. Admire
I must, and cannot quieten desire.

When every promise has been thinned
To nothing, there is still this bourne,
   White scorn
Between my enemies and one
Who would gladly have lied as they have done.

True-lips, and a tumescent tongue
Let no man call virtue. They are
   A bar
To my extravagance, a trip-wire
To my feet, in any courtship.

The bed lies empty, the great dung
Heap unshifted, because if any will
   Or skill
Is required, I am not the man.
Envy kiss-my-arse, only you can.

Aller Church

The art, the artifex, and I.
    Let the wind blow softly.
Currents of air over the plain.
    When shall I see England again?
The mouse creeps in the sedge. The fire runs
    Over the stubble against the sun.
This world is not yours. Walk here
    Under the half edge of Sedgemoor.

Van Dieman's Land

1.

Down
In the drink it
Might be called, for no
Reason but the best

There are no bearings down here
Nor instruments, the
Nauseous epidermes of mermaids do not
Through the transmarine darkness
Show any light.

It is hell and ham-bones, gnaw-
ing the specific meat,
In retreat
From all the world, like a squid
Into the sand,
Law
Sub-burrowed by a conjunctive and

It is no more than that and
The conjunction is not firm it
Waits
To establish nothing is
Variable as wind, flitting
Between cliff pillars of if and when,
Itself less and more uncertain.

What the sea
Dictates it answers
Amiss, or comes softly home
To the west windows, home
But does not enter. No
Voice could. There are daughters also
Of sea-urchins and the moved weeds
Who exceed, they say, in all beauty
But the crabs walk by them indifferent.
I have kept
Several seasons without endeavour
And slept.

II.

I do not see it
As others do
Nor shall anyone see
What indignity
Is to be suffered by love
Which alone
In the Crucifixion
Scarifies the bone.
A pauper walking to Henstridge
In a white coat,
Four tallies for feathers
And this I hope.
How many miles to Martock?
King-estrich toun
No mind for this kind
But the wind for seven.
This also be it said:
Van Dieman's Land,
Shackles upon the feet
And hand.
No answer from the exception
To any rule.
Each man his children
And a fool.

III.

The mind's
An elusive fish
In a deep pond.
Satan are you there?

Swimmingly.

In the Trojan Ditch

1. *Troilus and Cressida*

There is a mountain
Left forgotten
Under the uneasy eye of Dulcimer
I betray you? I, I, I?

Wizened with wisdom
The peat hair shagged over his brow
Armour is bright.
You to attempt me? Or who?

Basnet, basons of thunder, sword out
Elephantine in the extreme day
Night
For such encounters I say.
Helen
Troy down upon your altars.

Thus say all sages and I too
Vergil, necromancer, renounce Troy.
Aeneas sailing away, Dido is lost
To find one, Palinurus, your loss.

Sage Cressid, stain on your bed
The eye-glass in Pandar's eye
Uncle, how go maidenheads?

Dawn broke on the city, that day
Arches and battlements, the same
Light coming through them, the same.

II. *Helen*

The horse looks over the wall
Ulysses like a pack of monkeys
Is it the face or the arse?
Crude sufferers, a tail
Is worth a face.
It is the mind
Dallying through all the strings
From feet to toes
To hands to fingers all
To head
Curled in a smile part custom and part taste.
The walls
Are high
What is within
On flock beds, altars. Houses all
Contain the kernel of the savage world.
Go home Penelope
And Pelops line
Drawn through the centre, O.

III. *Athene*

Excoriate
Exaggerated, near dead
Racked, ripped
Uncovered, dismembered
The ribs
Cracked in a nut-cracker, the head
Opened with a tin-opener
The tongue
Extended like a flash tie
One eye
Turned upwards while
The other plays on a curved toe-nail.
This is my mercenary self
Also my best
Elegant, denuded, damned
Correctest

Extrapolation of fancy going inwards.
Outwards indeed
There is the epidermis, yours and yours
Form, measure, feet
Athene
Like a rock.

Ambition

Ambition is what fools remember;
Excise then from my mind the same,
The fruit whittled, the bough cast.

No mind now seek through the darkness
What mine has sought, and slewed away,
In youth love, in age content.

Ovid in Pontus

I am an old man whose death is foreseen,
Bystanders admire my longevity.
I see them eat every word I mean,
Yes, and excrete pity.
Di maris et coeli, what if the air
Is empty enough to receive prayer?
Do I have to pray? Because Pontic cold
Is under my cloak now that I am old?
It is under my skin, fashionable tears.
A suitable place to die, or to make amends;
Failure makes enemies as success friends.

Daphne

You cannot start a poem without a word.
    Speak none, for then the silence is absurd.
Even the fishes swim against the tide.
    And do you never want to be outside?
Great God, your prisoner weeps, and so do I.
    Miracles are arranged accordingly.
Ité, ité but you shall not go forth.
    Is it not prison for two pennyworth?
Sleep behind walls. There shall be sleep
    Revelatory as it shall be deep.
Two sides, two pillows. Truth lays its head on one.
    Is there another or shall love have none?
The body, yes. How shall it walk this way?
    Shall it be indiscriminate and pray?
Is love then over all? Are these trees
    Also cared for, oratory breeze?
They are of the flesh of the cross,
    Lignum, the wood he hung on; what he was,
Corpus & sanguis not to be saved alive.
    That so, would it not better be
To be metamorphosed Daphne?

Trafalgar Square

There is no remedy but death
And that you need not hanker for
For no obscure oblivion
Waits for your bones, but certain hope
Of coming to a blinding light,
Each part of you without pity
Remembered. No extreme failure
Not matched with desert; honey,
If it is for you at all, laid on your burns.
This is my belief, hardly to be reconciled
With that demure Saviour I apprehend
Somewhere among the shades. But all is mystery,
In pity of my understanding, not
To wrap myself in, here in Trafalgar Square.

The Crucifix

I go diminuendo all the time
    Towards a heap of dust or splash of slime.
All good is in the flesh, and what I see
    Answers to this description exactly.
But I must not touch, I must be blind
    To the exact image within my mind,
My ligaments trudge to destruction
    Between high walls. The resurrection
Will hoist me also before the judge
    I do not want to see, and my grudge-
Eaten mind be emptied before him.
    And yet the mind I shall have will be a limb
Of that great flesh of the risen Lord.
    How flesh? and how can it then afford
House-room for discontent? But I here
    Am subject to all want, though my gear
Cannot show any fraction of my needs
    But itch and scratch. It is for this God bleeds.
O crucifix, you are indeed my lust,
    You are the examination of my dust.
My mind perjures and twists while you cry
    Silently but so loud you tear the sky.
Wherefore these tears? Shall I rejoice?
    I would do, if I could hear your voice.

Pickers and Stealers

Pickers and stealers, my false friends,
    You have not served my ends.
No lack of malice on my part
    Holds you back. You lack art.
But here are people to admire:
    The delicate liar,
At home with treason like the cat;
    Softer than that,
The sleight-of-word who does not lie;
    The pleaser. What am I?
The man inclined to larceny
    Who stops at envy.

The Salad

To sordid death I go. Time after time
The days escape without fortune of rhyme
Or other incident of better wit.
No mind is manners, none is mine.
I am the epitome of slime,
Church furniture, slum wit, a card
Fallen from the pack. Mix me a salad.

Evening

Sleep has my muscles and a cord my throat.
Faint heart! The rooks at evening repair,
Climbing upon so many steps on air,
To the elm tops: caw, on the balustrade,
Caw from the church-tower, where the dead are laid
Under a passing shadow. I to tea,
Beside the fire in the old house, quietly.

The Discarnation

I.

The individual is the thing
Or it is either me or you.
        I do
Not care which way I sing
           This part
So long as I can somehow start.

There are two ways of looking at
The subject, either from within,
          As in
A scallop, diving bell or hat,
           Or slope
The eyes up through a telescope.

They are two different animals,
It sometimes seems, the man
          Who can
Reflect, and does, the swaying walls
           And he
Who sways himself for all to see.

For to be seen and stir within
The porridge of the consciousness
          Is less
One action than to flash a fin
           And sink
Down to the bottom of the ink.

The seen continuum of act
Of something else, makes that a thing.
          A wing
Or speaking head is doubtless fact
           And far
More so than you can show you are.

But the observer is observed,
You think. He is not. What you see
          Is me

As something linear, straight or curved,
        Which I,
As I, should certainly deny.

Though all the time, to understand,
Men make a certain sort of face
        Or pace
Impatiently, or lift a hand
        To greet
Another pair of travelling feet,

Yet this proves nothing. Every look
Is attribution. What I see
        Can be
So little more than what I took
        Before
As imprints on my mind's clean floor.

From what? What passes there? All ghosts?
Or able spirits like my own?
        The moan
The tree makes touches me, the hosts
        Of eyes
Around me also sympathise

– And I with them. A comity
Is what we make for comfort's sake
        To break
Our prison, not to be let free
        But bind
Some obligation on our mind.

For our supremest wish, ourself,
Must find its equal, or we die.
        The sky
Is peopled; Ghibbeline and Guelf
        Stick out
Of history books like a pig's snout.

And we admit companionship
In people passing in the street.

        The beat
Suggests the heart, likewise the quip
        The mind
Which, multiplied, makes out mankind.

While these unsure companions dance
Before our eyes, we can forget
        The set
They move in is our glance,
        The tears
They shed a humming in our ears.

Also forget that, worst of all,
There is no bottom to our well.
        To tell
What is reflected there, what wall
        Is there
We peer into a breathless air.

But whether in or out, or who
It is that peers, one does not know.
        A flow
Of sorts is there; there are some few
        Dark bits
That float on what are called our wits.

But I is not found there. It is
Not found at all. Descartes
        Was smart
Enough to catch a glimpse of his
        But since
A cogitat has only been a wince.

Conscience perhaps? Or consciousness?
A pool of that is not a man.
        What can
The lizard say? And yet the guess
        Is that
He sees, although perhaps non cogitat.

And the computer reads my cheques
And thinks as well as you or me.
        Maybe
Our calculus is more complex;
        Its trick
A variant of arithmetic.

But number is concealed in verse
And every preference we show.
        We know
The good from better, bad from worse
        Without
Counting what brought the choice about.

Or do we count but, like machines
Simply not notice what we do?
        Have you,
Choosing a summum bonum, seen
        The hands
Clock up the number of the sands?

The things we notice are a spot
Of light in a dark countryside.
        The wide
Part is unknown but not
        Unten-
anted by animals and men,

Alive and dead. The small part is
What passes for the mind of man
        Or can
Be seen upon its surfaces,
        A glade
In which he dances unafraid.

How came the mind to be that shape?
Or there at all? How first the axe
        Made cracks
In that wide forest, how the nape
        First said
The word that grew into the head:

All that is Logos, and obscure.
The shape is history. A mind
        Will find
The way it has been taught. Past cure,
        It sees
No hope except in its disease.

And when you think you are yourself
It is a kind of learned joke.
        You croak
A dead man's words, take from the shelf
        A book
In which all generations look

And read a line which two or three
Imagine they have made their own,
        Though known,
With variants, throughout history.
        A form
Of language is a human norm

And it is made in several styles,
As, 'Dozōō' in the Japanese
        For 'Please'
(Used sometimes in the British Isles)
        Which may
Mean 'Bitte' or else 'S'il vous plaît.'

That is the simplest proof there is
That similar is not the same.
        The name,
Likewise, of Gert or Bert or Liz
        Conceals
Less difference than the subject feels.

And everything we do is form
Of manner, language or physique.
        The meek
And violent equally are norms
        And we
Are less than our mythology.

Yet what we think is less, for sure,
Than what we are, and that is flesh.
        Its fresh
Bloom is the best we know. Its dure
        Descent
The hardest way that we are sent.

It starts in comfort, or at least
It does not know it is a start.
        A part
Unwittingly and, when released,
        It finds
One body has become two minds.

Whether its first thought comes with breath
Depends on what you mean by thought;
        But caught
In air, it feeds on it till death
        And takes
As sauce the ripples the air makes.

Its softness becomes strength, its coos
Turn into words and bite. Its sex
        Will vex
Itself and everything it woos.
        Its eyes
Will see the world and show surprise.

But youth once lost, a lizard skin
Envelops organs with a twist.
        All's missed
That called the appetite within.
        Pretence
At last replaces every sense.

To die is best at last, and yet
The last kick struggles after life.
        The knife
That enters like a prince is met
        By will
Which is the last thing to be still.

II.

As I approach my second theme
Decorum stares me in the face.
        No place
For ribaldry or pretty dream
        Which lure
The senile and the immature.

Man is conventional, he lives
According to imagined laws.
        The cause
Is partly in himself who gives
        The rule;
In part they are discovered by the fool.

Confused between discovery
And natural error of the heart,
        By art
He finds he may be free;
        By right
Searches the arrow of his flight.

Two bodies in one mind – the mark
If any, of the lover's knot –
        And not
As something hollowed in the dark,
        But found
As paradise to build around.

And if this cannot be, the flesh,
Which is not dildo or mere meat,
        Will bleat
Outside another mind's thin mesh
        Till cross-
petition makes a general loss.

Or, falling back upon themselves,
Each mind admits the other's fears.
        Then tears
Pour out over eroded shelves
        As of
The dried-up torrent-bed of love.

When they are spent the stones are seen.
There is an end of all soft charm.
       The harm
That lovers do has always been
       The mind,
More calculating then than kind.

And if one mind two bodies touch,
— But not the two of unity —
       The he
Both him and her, and she as much
       Both her
And him, they are not as they were.

No innocence, deliberate love,
Pleasure, but not the blinded hope,
       The slope
But not the precipice above
       The prec-
ipice, high above emptiness.

The body turned to instrument?
As if it could be! But that lie
       Will try
To turn the drift of each intent
       And wear
A face that's slightly more than fair.

And so the flesh betrays the mind
And must be guarded like a jewel,
       So cruel
It is when it is unconfined
       And yet
Imprisoned, it is overset,

Bedevilled, peeved. But bond or free
Are parables of servitude,
       While prude
And lecher both are equally
       Without
The key that lets the body out.

Because the body is the mind
To speak of gaolers is absurd.
        The word
Is friend, the blind leading the blind.
        And so
In tears the man and woman go.

They were not always in one yoke.
They issued out of separate wombs,
        The tombs
Of separate affections, broke
        In fear
Into a separate atmosphere

And lived for years without their sex
Or with so little that the heart
        Was part
Of everything and could annex
        A tree
As well as an identity.

Then doubt and reason grew a twig
On branches formed of love and hate.
        A late
Comer was lust, who is so ig-
        norant
Because it does not hear, and can't.

If lust had raised its roaring voice
Before the mind had formed its ring
        Nothing
Could have withstood it, and no choice
        Been made,
Or else it would have been afraid.

But as it grew, provoked by mind,
By whom it was contained, it caught
        The thought
(Which, nascent, is so near combined
        With flesh)
And so drove on to lust afresh.

The intellectual pursuit
Of all, desire then became.
        The name
Was often changed, although the root
        Remained
And sap in everything complained.

So adolescence turned into
A trap for ingenuity.
        The key
Of everything it tried to do
        Was lust
It would not own unless it must.

So hearts and heads and other parts
Became confused. Analysis
        Which is
So bright, picked out the darts
        Which hurt
And then the youth became alert.

His object then, through thick and thin,
Was much and falsely simplified.
        He cried
For certain patches of bare skin –
        But, kind,
Paid his addresses to the mind.

More wise than he, his elders then
Obstructed all that he essayed
        And made
A ritual with a long amen,
        The which
Denatured quite his primal itch.

But gave him a society,
Anxious and troubled all his life,
        A wife
In whose routine embraces he
        Might find
A body had become a mind.

This practice for paternal love
Employed his economic strength.
        At length
He'd house and crockery to prove
        The plan
Is more important than the man.

Then children came to make complete
His service to the commonwealth.
        By stealth
We have good done to us. We eat
        The food
Others prepared for their own good.

Since every thought must have its act
And not all thought begins inside,
        The wide
Extension of a private fact
        Will give
The failed man an excuse to live.

He fails because there is no man
Except in number and exchange.
        The range
Of one man's mind in no way can
        Invent
A world in which a life is spent.

And there are engines make us go
Without our knowledge. So the mind
        Confined
To what we tell ourselves we know
        Is ill
Accomplished to direct the will

And does not do so. And the heart,
So-called, is only a vague belt
        Of felt
Impressions, so a dimmer part
        Of the
Same instrument of cecity.

But facts and bodies operate
Upon our whims and so we are.
        The jar
Of honey and the sting don't wait
        Till you
Imagine hives, and flowers in dew

Or the digestion or the cure.
The world is ready-made and we
        Who see
And taste and smell are too unsure
        To make
Any resolve but a mistake.

No reason therefore to despise
A little magic in your drink
        Or think
That antiseptic thoughts comprise
        The best
And highest that can be expressed.

Reflect: the first, near-simian men
Put in their rods without a thought.
        They sought
And found, but knew it no more when
        They'd done
Than omne animal post coitum.

The second men observed there was
An act worth taking notice of,
        Though love
Is not imputed to this phase,
        Indeed,
Nor the analogy of seed.

The third men noticed, very sly,
That nine moon cycles brought a birth
        Though earth
And air might have to join the cry.
        But still
They knew the act was not the will.

The fourth man is the Onan-Stopes
(The latter the more technical
        But all
The same in terms of fears and hopes
        – Technique,
However, makes the hope more weak).

Children are born through platitude,
Error or love or anything,
        The spring,
Long winter evenings, or mood
        Or al-
cohol, the same moons bring them all.

And, having come, like stars themselves,
They govern others' destinies
        But ease
No favour in their own behalves
        For love
Comes from around if not above.

So, drawn out by these facts, the man
Who acts the part of father finds
        That minds
Grow in and out of things, and can
        Be grown
Like lichen on from stone to stone.

III.

And so with place. A habitat
Is habit in a certain space,
        A face
With thought behind. It seems like that
        And who
Shall say it has less thought than you?

Places have names because a thought
Lives in them, changing like our own
        And grown
Wily with years, not to be caught,
        So meant
Only by words we don't invent.

Cerne Abbas is a name I like;
Toller Porcorum even more.
        Ebbor
Valley by Priddy has a psych
        -e which
Can be counted to make you twitch.

It is painful that men should die
And be forgotten. Places prove
        That love
Or even hatred will long try
        Not to
Be, and names are to remind you.

If you sit on a barrow and
Play your transistor, still the dead
        Will head
Their way out of the ground, the hand
        Which slew
Your ancestor will be on you.

It does not matter if you don't
Feel it, it is certainly there.
        You dare
Admire yourself because you don't
        And close
Your eyes upon the dead man's toes.

Your ignorance does not seal up
The innumerable petitions.
        The guns
Emplaced upon the coast still plop
        The shell
Into the sea although you are well.

Thomas Tusser still ploughs these hills
Though you may not have heard of him.
        You trim
Your smile to contemporary wills.
        Who said
That you too would not join the dead?

They are living, as well as you;
And their thoughts creep into your bones.
      Rough stones
May have more to say that is true
      Than men
Who do not know how to say Amen.

Labour instead of thought will do
To form the man, for what he makes
      Soon takes
Its part in shaping me and you.
      We are
The subtlest artifacts by far.

The house that grows upon a hill
Remembers like the hill itself.
      The self
Which likes to think it is a will
      Is but
The image of an acre and a hut

And certain kind words spoken too
Before it knew what they could mean.
      The seen
Enters beside the heard, the true
      Image
Burrows inside the living rage.

That is the man. The furrows eat
His aching brain out as he ploughs.
      To rouse
Him there is the sun. To greet
      His bit-
-ter end there is the mud pit.

Happy if between rise and fall
Some creature greets him for a day
      And clay
Cakes on his boots and a few tall
      Trees rise
Before him to excite surprise.

He is happy indeed if such
As Salisbury spire teach him to expect
      Direct
Fruition outside his own hutch.
      This is
The best of man's artifices.

But number has replaced intent
For most; they are not cattle they
      Betray
The heritage of cattle, bent
      On what
They think they cannot say is not

But no more attentive to what is
Than a sewing-machine to cloth,
      And loth
To reject an analysis
      Which tells
At least how to avoid bad smells

And ensures that they die in peace
In well-furnished euthenasia.
      These are
The objectives of our police
      Although
It does not always work out so.

Quiconque meurt, meurt à douleur
– Or so it used once to be said.
      The dead
Do not report on it. There were
      No doubt
Once more who screamed as they went out.

Do not under-rate benefits
Everybody seeks to enjoy
      The boy
Shut away because out of his wits;
      Foetus
Smothered lest it should bother us.

We are the heirs of an emptiness
Of which we are extremely proud;
        The crowd
Soothed as it never was, a less
        Extreme
Nightmare, and a less hopeful dream.

And artifacts less regarded
Then ever before, because made
        For trade
And not for use, and by the dead
        Hand of
Number instead of by our love.

Not even made to be consumed
As is sometimes said. Made so that
        The rat
In the sewer is well groomed;
        The count
Of nothing will continually mount.

Over the hills now there advance
The artifacts, both man and thing,
        A string
Choking the leaders of the dance;
        Their blood
Cannot do their brains any good.

So, departing into Thing
As if the Pied Piper had called them,
        The hem
Of the garment is untouched, to sing
        Is not
Necessary, and that's my lot.

Hactenus Arvorum Cultus

Up to now the fields
Have been ploughed and the stars
Sent us home to our cottages
At the end of the day.
There has been the vine,
Even on these hills, and the slow
Growing olive.
Not only the Cotswold shepherd
But I too, with even pace,
Treading where the wind can be heard
Or some horn perhaps. But this is over.
Not even metal ringing
At the smithy, or a voice.
Water sucking the rotting
Piers,
The algae lifted
Tide by tide.
A single gull
Banking, back to the dead sea,
Cries.

Palaestra and Ampelisca

It was the first foot that came ashore.
The whoremaster with the brilliant eye
Remained on board, the waves ran skeltering in.
Then the ship broke and the whoremaster
Lumbered after the girls. The two ran
With wet garments baffling their slippery bodies.
The girls had been intended for pleasure in Sicily
But things do not work out as men intend.

Anacreon

Men have their animosity
And women have what they can give,
Beauty, unless you choose to call
Their presence by another name.
Nothing is new. Anacreon
Said 'crumple swords and put out flames.'

Hod Hill

Ovid, you are too slack. I can see the hill,
Hod Hill in Dorset, where you had your camp –
So I may call it, in sympathy. The natives
Came streaming over the walls. Like birds, you said,
A flight of ill omen, carrying off
Tomorrow's dinner perhaps, even tonight's.
It may be. Your horror was even more,
That walking in the streets there were no Romans.
Even the Greeks were suspect, chatting with savages
In their own language. Over half the houses
Were native-owned. The rough, the treacherous.
Arrows were found in the streets, far from the walls.
No security here. Look back, dear Ovid,
On Rome to fall, but not in your day.

No Address

In my leprosy I have lost speech
Which before I had with several.
Now no voices, not even my own.

Pliny, Horace, Cicero, talk to me;
I am a dead language also.
The poetry owners cannot make me out

Nor I them. And the big mouths of learning
Open and close over my thoughts without biting.
Under the shadow of politics I have no teeth.

I am no man, Caesar, to stand by you,
Nor have the whimsical humour of pre-war Oxford
But my unrecognised style was made by sorrow.

Inching towards death, let me go there quickly.
Silently, in the night or in the day-time,
Equally, I would take it like a Roman.

For Patrick Swift

The dishes are untouched
And yet I see them all
Spread out under the moon.

Quiet, which nothing spoils,
Not even appetite,
Hung on the point of wish.

Milk-white, with ruddy fruit
Only the angry heart
Is mean enough to ask.

Ice in the silver night
With the bird voices held
In silver cups, tonight.

Human Relations

My mind is so evil and unjust
I smile in deprecation when I am flattered
But inside the palace of my smile
Is the grovelling worm that eats its own tail
And concealed under the threshold of my lips
Is the trustless word that will wrong you if it can.
Come nearer to me therefore, my friend,
And be impressed by the truth of my explanation.
No less, lady, take my chaste hand
While the other imaginatively rifles your drawers.

Virgini Senescens

I.

Do you consider that I lied
Because I offered silent hands?

And are my lips no use at all
Unless they have a lie to tell?

Because my eyes look doubtfully
Must they not look on you at all?

And if my hands drop to my sides
Are they then empty of desire?

And are my legs unusable
Because the linked bones of my feet

Rest where they are upon the floor?
I could have used them otherwise

And brought my legs across the room,
Lifted my arms and caught you up

And housed my eyes under your brows
And fixed my lips upon your own.

Or would you then have said that I
Performed but did not speak the truth?

II.

Although the body is your truth
The mind may have some part in it

As, mine that holds your body fast
And yours, said to keep house inside

Perhaps the yawning mind of God
Which folds us in his universe.

The mind that holds you is my eye
The quicksilver inside your own

Which, seeing me, collects and runs;
It is the mucous in my skull

And your intestines tight with fear
Our several secret, hirsute parts

Our finger-nails which dig the flesh;
It is our flushed or dented skin

The toes we clench inside our shoes.
Or do you think it less than that?

The spidery numbers you can read?
The tricks they play among themselves?

The art by which you hope to draw
A self from chaos, and be pleased?

A reputation? Who admires?
Oh, I am old and sly, I twist

A way through ribs and weeds and trees
And mark my body as I go:

While you are young, and hardly dare
Moisten your lips upon a stone,

Your fluttering look is hardly out
And does not reach your nearest parts.

Do not imagine I am bold.
It is this terror I admire:

It is the shaking universe
I too inhabit, but in me

Age has reformed the hope of love.
The *quia impossibile*

Drifts with me as, I make no doubt,
It travels with the astronaut.

III.

I turn myself from you, to think
Upon the gravity of age

Which bears upon me now until
My weightless body floats in space.

I want it anchored where I live
Why should I bother with the mind?

It is an old excuse for death
Or else a young man's sleight-of-hand:

Attend to that and he will grow
And, silent as a savage, steal

Upon the world of sex and war.
He will grow up while I grow down

And hold you firmly in his arms
Still talking of the intellect

And, turning to me, will pretend
That we are equals in our minds

Although my body shrink until
He well could throw me out of doors

Or push my huddled frame against
The fender, while he pokes the fire.

It has not come to that, but I
Must plan now my civilities

While I can give him knock for knock.
I will accept his gambit and

Use all my thin and polished words
To make him feel my harmless ease

Whereas my burning heart prepares
To snatch you from him if I can.

It can do you no good, this war
In which you gain by my defeat.

Do not suppose I shall give up
Till I have hurt you if I can.

Iago was an honest man;
I have that reputation too.

Eurydice

If I took your maidenhead
As I well might do,
Softly to Acheron
I would go down.
Parting the rushes there:
'Where are the King and Queen
Of this fell kingdom? Has
Love any part in it?'
Striking the lyre,
Orpheus in every inch.
'If the legend is true
It has some part. Proserpine
Was fetched here from the fields,
April bore her in love.
This reign, so long,
Over the bloodless dead
Began with love.'
And the King with pity:
'You shall have her if you can
And not look back.'
Softly, past the sedge,
I drew back. Eurydice!
Faint words come from you.
When you stretch your hand
It is hardly air you catch,
One voice between us
Hangs and is lost.
Eurydice!
Retracted now. The gates.

Seven days beside the Styx
Orpheus sat, without corn
Wine of any country
No food but tears.
Within the gates of the dead
Eurydice. Weeping,
If there can be tears.
Orpheus goes back to Thrace,
In those hard mountains
Learns to hate all women.
For her, it might be said
But that is false.

The Rope

Now money is the first of things
And after that the human heart
Which beats the time it can afford.
      What springs
    Of passion, what a smart
        Appearance, Lord!
And are these spiritual things?

They are. And we that are without
Have failed to use the currency
Correctly. For we have allowed
      A doubt
    About the things we see
      To sing aloud
And put our calculations out.

If the external is the hope
We have here, as I think it is,
We should respect it till we die.
      The slope
    Is steep, the precipice
      Is near. And I
Now know that money is the rope.

The Garden of Epicurus

My heart was evil but I did no wrong.
Then I designed a way of doing evil.
Smiling was my first fault. I counted myself pleasant,
Which I am not. And from this there grew
Several keen ways of extruding evil.
My eyes shot glances and I salivated;
My words came like honey and I was just.
Soon I had the rewards of this conduct.
Every endeavour was made to please me.
The mind felt like a sovereign in its own weight.
They were fortunate who knew me. Until no resemblance
Remained to the man who licked the sores of the world
– Admittedly a filthy practice but I think now as wholesome
As anything the successful get up to.
It may be that happiness is a sign of evil.

The Person

What is the person? Is it hope?
If so, there is no I in me.
    Is it a trope
Or paraphrase of deity?
    If so,
I may be what I do not know.

Do not be proud of consciousness
For happiness is in the skin.
    What you possess
Is what another travels in.
    Your light
Is phosphorus in another's night.

It does not matter what you say
For any what or who you are
    Is of a day
Which quite extinguishes your star –
    Not speech
But what your feelers cannot reach.

There is one God we do not know
Stretched on Orion for a cross
    And we below
In several sorts of lesser loss
    Are we
In number not identity.

Every Reality is a Kind of Sign

The self is the bit that has not yet emerged;
It is therefore completely unknowable.
It is perfect before the discovery of sex.
When sex is known and the children have grown up
What blindness remains to me? And I cannot live without it.
There is only the dark arcanum of religion,
I prowl round the outside and am not let in.
Every reality is a kind of sign.

The Recollection

In darkness I set out,
    O solstice of my year!
Mindful, though I had none,
    Of crowding ancestors.
And yet I grew in fear
    Although in love also.
The dogs yelped in the street;
    I would not run from them.
Terror and love held still
    The balance where I stood.
Terror pulled down the sky
    But love inclined my feet.
My seedling year grew great
    But did not touch its spring
Unless beside the brooks
    I followed to their source
Or under sprouting ferns
    Or the pale cowslip-cups.
My mind had spread until

It covered up the sky;
No art could make it wince
    Though sleep would hold it fast.
How long this wakeful dream
    Engulfed me, who can say?
The busy heart beat on
    Until I heard it knock
And then my flesh spoke out:
    'Break through the silken sheet
That hangs before the world
    And bellies in the wind.'
Not I, not I for fear
    Or was it also love?
Or recollection of
    A world more beautiful?
And yet at last a rent
    Came in that silken veil
And, neither in nor out,
    I struggled for my life.
Where has my life passed since?
    In tatters, thorns and shreds,
Under the briar I creep;
    The puddle is my drink.
The pebbles in the path
    Are my extremest stars.
Who treads that Milky Way?
    Some giant, but not I.
I am the broken chalk
    Under his foot, the twig
That lies across his path.
    High summer came and went;
I did not find my God
    Although my body bore
The impress of a cross,
    Faint, almost negligible.
And now the autumn comes
    With pounding strides, and day
Closes her weary eye,
    I find no trace of peace
Nor vigour for the war
    And God looks down upon

One who does not look up.
   The heavens, which held my mind,
Have closed, and left me small.
   Saint Thomas now brings in
My last and shortest day.
   I seek my terminal.
The candle gutters fast.
   Along the corridor
The last footfall is lost.
   There is no friend but God;
On him I may presume
   Because He does not come.
O could I have that mind
   I carried in the womb,
Which knew, but could not say,
   This solstice would be birth.

The Alley-Way

I have come to a great blank wall.
There is no escape through either alley-way,
To left or right. Standing on each corner
Are youth and beauty, changed as in a mirror,
Their skirts modishly short. If I were beginning again
I would not eat my heart out for any woman.
Yet that was life. A cloud of unknowing.
Knowledge by comparison is a thin thing,
A smile of evil spread over the face of the world.

I hear a footfall
And turning hope to see someone on the pavement.
The footfall has gone.
If this were a long road it would still be empty
For hope is also an echo.
There is no way in fact out of my dream.

The Withdrawal

Also that you should not withdraw,
As you have now done, or so it seems,
Into the recesses of pain,
Was also a reason why your superficies
Seemed to me as important as your eyes.
Now that Diana has gone, your eyes' Actaeon
It is that my dogs pursue to tear you to bits.

The Spectre

He was born, I should think, under a star
Towed into position by an astronaut,
        Not caught
By the malice of remote constellations, as many are

– Between the jaws of Leo or the pincers of the Crab,
Or pushed along by a bellowing Taurus.
        Sagittarius
Did not riddle him. He did not suffer under the grab

Of Scorpio, was not twinned by Gemini.
Aries did not butt him or Virgo make him promises
        Nor was his
Effigy weighed by Libra. Nor did he

Weep with Aquarius, swim dumbly with the Fish
Or stink excessively with Capricorn.
        He was born
To see out his days with credit and relish.

His birth was antiseptic, though accidental
And after the misconception, the die ran straight.
        No great
Event shattered his uterine life, but all

Went more or less as the clinic would direct.
There was just room for the advice he got
        And not
Enough for anything one did not expect.

His final emergence was of course timely,
His statistics those you will find in the text-books;
        His looks
Neither well nor ill, he was simply a baby

And persisted in that role for the suitable time.
Every age of childhood followed in due order.
        There were
No complications about weaning. His prime

Condition indeed stayed with him till the end
As if he had been a piece for the butcher's block.
        The lack of shock
In his history was just what had been planned.

After the gynaecologists, the paediatricians;
In the end a model for geriatrics.
        In the six-
-ty years between he was treated with entertainments.

I do not want to go so fast, however.
There was I am glad to say paedobaptism
        – An ism
Added to the list not for science but for the air

It gave and in the hope that it would influence
His sexual morals, as you might geld a cat.
        But that
Again is getting a little in advance.

I will not tell you how he played with his excreta
But he knew well enough he had to go through that stage.
        At the age
Psychologists said he should stop, he did. Ah,

He was good as gold. I cannot remember
In what order these vices come, but they do.
        He got through
The lot in exemplary fashion, whatever they were.

His kindergarten was one long game, or they said it was
And he showed no disposition to contradict.
        They did not inflict
Any blow more painful than a Beta minus.

After that he became quite a little man
– A form prefect, and obedient in the scrum.
        His bum
Was occasionally kicked, which gives manners if anything can.

Elementary Christianity and economics,
Some French, a few experiments called science
        In defiance
Of ignorant traditions which preferred the classics.

You cannot found a mind but you can eradicate
Superstition by such means, or so it is said.
        Anyhow it led
To admittance, through the Ivory or Plastic Gate

To one of our superior universities.
His studies were, predictably, in Modern Affairs,
        The bears
And bulls of the market rather than of the mythologies.

He committed fornication, but with discretion;
Spoke fluently and well, but about nothing.
        He would even sing,
Music being part of the embalming lotion.

What eminently learned men cultivated his mind!
It was a treat to see how smooth they made him,
        So trim
About the edges and what emptiness behind!

He was a tabula rasa, but not quite.
There was a faint trace of liberal opinion;
        The Guardian
Was his newspaper, which was of course right.

Need I tell you that he thought for Him Self
About abortion, euthanasia, even religion?
        What fun
To take down a new idea from the shelf!

Naturally he was suitable for the best employments
Where every cultivation is required.
        He was hired
By an advertising agency to write copy, which he enjoyed.

And so began to write for the weeklies
– It was longer you see, and the goods he had to recommend
        In the end
Even less durable, needing imagination as well as critical faculties.

Do not suppose that his personal life
Was neglected among these services to culture.
        The lure
Of experiment had faded at the right time, and he had a wife.

A little more steady with the contraceptives
Than his parents were, his children came when they were called,
        Not appalled
By the prospect of the life which such a father could give.

The tabula was pretty rasa already
But he was determined to rase it further.
        His motives were
Understood and seconded by his wife, so it was easy.

The family lived in accordance with all the graphs
While the children were young. Also when they were old
        For he was bold
And sought freedom with another woman, which is a laugh.

He wrote books, I cannot tell you how many;
They were reviewed, praised, and rapidly sank from sight.
        As was right
His opinions were often heard on the B.B.C.

Big enough in the mouth for a life peer,
He became one of the chief clowns of our public life,
        His second wife
Clinging on to the outside without a trace of fear.

However, he died, like the rest of us,
A soul in torment, an obituary in *The Times*.
        As he climbs
He finds the universe unexpectedly spacious.

He was last seen passing by Aldebaran
And had a long journey to go after that.
        God sat
Waiting for him, as you may suppose, with a prepared judgment.

It was the surprise of his life, you might say;
For once he had no opinion to express
        – A less
Cruel deprivation than he supposed, on Judgment Day.

We who remain below, though not for long,
Cannot hope to surpass this man in vacuity
        But we
May prudently join the angels in a song:

        'Existence is
        Not what you say,
        Which does not count
        On Judgment Day;
        It is not even
        What you think,
        Which is but a
        Deceptive link
        Between your God
        And what you are
        – And what that is
        Is far from clear.
            So, Alleluia! loudly raise
            A song of ignorance and praise.'

The Regrets

I.
Beware of age.
For I have learned
An old man should
Be kept in chains.
He is a gentle
Psychopath;
The passion that
He had is dead.
His youthful walk
And grey moustache
Conceal a heart
Which cannot feel.
The courtesy
Which he expends
Is poison to
His younger friends.
His virtues are
A kind of shell
To keep him cosy
In his skull.
I tell you mark
This leper well
And send him forward
With a bell.

II.
Young men are fools
And now I am old
I am a fool.

III.
Lust is the star
Which lit my way
And brought me close
To where you lay
– One wise man with
A pack of lies
Or not enough

To make him wise.
God's blood, they say,
Oozed from the tree.
The serpent sweated
Just like me
But in his more
Enlightened years
The devil was
A gentleman.

The Cave

The human mind is deeper than had been supposed;
It is the same depth as the human body
– That is why I value the soles of your feet
And am only moderately impressed by your eyes.
Your thoughts may be examined at all your entrances.

Yet the very name of thought promises a delineation
Which is not that of any or of the sum of your members.
I am horrified that this ghost inhabits you,
But it is this which brings you into these caverns
I live in. You move towards me across the wet floor.

Can we speak, except in terms of our bodies
And is that language available to us?
Where does speech come from? Is someone addressing us?
Is what we speak what we hear?
Cloud with misunderstanding in my arms.

The Shape

The passions are the shape of man.
I put it on a drawing-board.

Show the integument drawn back.
Draw pity round about the heart.

Pity is small and avarice
No bigger, where the nostrils curl

But envy goes from top to toe
And lust runs from the radial point

Into the tip of every limb
And every hair upon the head

And sorrow blackens out the lines
Of every hope; and deep despair

Gathers like bile above the groin
Until it fills the abdomen.

Lucky the shape was sketched before
I drew back the integument.

On the Coast

Thirty years ago I stood here,
Almost naked on the windy beach:
This is the body in which passion has decayed.

This is the clear water that sidled past me,
The white cliff, I can see it for a moment
I have no other authority for drowning.

This is certainly the body I left upon the shore
I found it the other day, crisped against the sea-weed:
This is the house in which I have slumbered these many years.

And now beside the water, walking close to the foam's edge
Before the grey turf, green turf and the brown corn-lands
I am wandering happily as an unidentified image.

But the mind will be applied in far-away London,
Bent over my files, residue of my spirit
The coming and going of thousands: it is a market-place.

I had not imagined anything but a blind future
And that is still with me, still beckoning onwards
Till the voices die and I am at rest.

It does not matter at that point what you do with my bones
These hills can have them or the dustman
So long as Dorset can brood over its grey sea.

The Queen of Lydia

Candaules, King of Lydia,
Whose mouth was bigger than his prick

Boasted about the Queen his wife:
'You ought to see her in her bath;

She is a smasher.' Gyges said
He thought it inappropriate.

He was a soldier and he knew
The elements of discipline.

He also knew you did not trust
A master with an outsized mouth.

The King insisted, and arranged
Gyges should stand behind the door

While she came in and got undressed.
And this he did. Candaules lay

Discreetly in his double bed,
His nose above the counterpane.

He liked the Queen to take her time
And put her folded garments on

A bench some distance from the bed,
Then strut about the room a bit.

All this she did; and Gyges watched.
Was his mind on his duty then?

He shook as he stood by the door.
As the Queen turned her lovely back

He made a noise and then went out.
Alas, he was not quick enough.

The Queen said nothing; she was sly
And thought instead and went to sleep.

Next day she sent for Gyges and
He trembled as behind the door.

She gave him this alternative:
'One of you two goes to the pot.

Either you kill the shameless king
And lie beside me in his bed

And also govern Lydia
Or I will have him murder you.'

The choice was easy: no one dies
Rather than sleep beside a girl.

And the Queen's motive? She believed
(The Lydians are barbarians)

To be seen naked was a shame
Which only death could expiate

Or marriage, as in Gyges' case.
So you see how barbarians are.

The Adventurer

When the sun was shining and the back door was open
He went indoors and successively raped seven women.
My own desires are not much different
Since I have given up the desire of understanding
And have not succeeded in ousting my other desires.
He wept and screamed in the dock. So would not I,
But my heart is armoured by intellection;
My heart has been hardened:
On that account I catch my trains with precision
And know how to look after myself, mate.

The Affirmative

The trick of sex, there is no doubt,
First taught the animals to speak.

But Yes is not a word at all;
The first word that they spoke was No.

All conversation still remains
A gloss upon the negative.

For Yes could only hold its tongue;
Its work is in another place.

On my Fifty-First Birthday

I.
Hare in the head-lights dance on your hind legs
Like a poor cat straggling at a rope's end.
Everything is cruelty for innocence.
If you could mark this escape from death
In your thin mind you would have eaten what I have
And, running from form to form, you would consider
The immeasurable benignity of the destructive God.

II.
A great sunlit field full of lambs.
The distant perspectives are of the patched earth
With hedges creeping about. If I were to die now
No need of angels to carry me to paradise.
O Lord my God, simplify my existence.

III.
The whole hill-side is roofed with lark-song.
What dangerous declivities may I not descend?
It is dark green where the horses feed.
Blackthorn and gorse open before my eyes.

IV.
The gulls come inland, alight on the brown land
And bring their sea-cries to this stillness.
It was waves and the surf running they heard before
And now the lark-song and the respiration of leaves.

In Brewer Street

You had better imagine who you are
As you cross Brewer Street diagonally
If you do not, darkness will fall.

In mind is consequence and sequence,
Importance – ah, my dear, perhaps being –
You cannot creep under that coverlet

Or you could cross the street and re-enter the stones
As if you disappeared between the mortar.
I could not love you without necessity

Nor could my hand touch yours without its ghost.
I do not want it, though I want you extremely.
Neither can meet, unless we consent to be there.

Horatius

It is annoying when your sister doesn't appreciate you.
Besides, the sweat of the fighting had been considerable
And Horatius was genuinely tired;
Only in killing could he find more energy
So he put his sword to the throat of the silly girl.
She met him coming with the spoils of the Curiatii upon him
At the Capena gate: the battle had been uncertain –
Two lots of triplets fighting out there, with the hosts
Looking on eagerly as at television
Their eyes following the preliminary javelins like tennis balls
And gasps escaping when they came to blows.
At first two of the Horatii were down
But not before they had wounded the three Curiatii.
Then Horatius had pretended to fly.
The three wounded Curiatii had limped after him
Single file and at considerable distances
And he had turned and done for them one by one.
The last had hardly fought, it was just a killing
So he was quite ready when he met his sister.
Also, her body was a soft one.
The people have no conception of justice
(And he had been so good on the television).
They made him walk under a beam hood-winked
As a sort of bogus expiation of murder
And Numa's successor thought he had better keep quiet.

Adam

I will go and visit the deer
They and the cat being my main accompaniments,
As it happens, in the silence which succeeds work.
The sunlight whitens the top of the chestnuts,
Bare for winter, and the snow
Blazes to gold. The cat is safe in the house.
Out there under the magnificent beeches
The deer have classified themselves according to sex.
Not creatures of man's invention
Still they nuzzle or walk where he has put them.
I, creature of God, am among man's artifacts.
With the beasts I creep into another day.
Nothing commands me to a particular form;
But for my name and address I might be water
Running into a puddle for the cat to lick
Or perhaps stretching its ripples in the sunlight
Among the frosted grass, for the deer to stale.
I acknowledge freely that I am part of the creation
But doubt whether I am a particle for whom salvation was intended.
My sympathy is with Adam
Walking in the garden in the cool of the day.
To avoid is best.
ADAM: But that was in fact not exactly my problem.
Like you of course I admitted I was created
– In my case it was self-evident;
God was always about like the breath of my nostrils.
Moreover I was, next him, the lord of the garden
And had given names to the animals one by one
As he presented them to me. It was because none of these
Seemed more than a rustle of the grasses through which they came
That I was presented with Eve. And I was astonished.
There was a new element of correspondence
Not perceptible then in the beasts, though now you see it.
The foolishness of the apron of fig-leaves
Was a first effort to rid myself of that.
When God called there was some confusion.
It was the first time he had spoken so loudly.
I thought he was another kind of Eve,
A more powerful Adam perhaps, like myself.

The conversation that followed was hallucinatory.
It is easy for you to laugh at our evasions.
The future was unsettled.
I decided to walk out of Eden and go to work.
Since then nothing has been clear.
If I see Paradise it is between branches,
A glimpse over the cooking-pot while Cain and Abel
Quarrel over a skin.
It has been very interesting to meet you.
Somewhere between us is the second Adam.

Homo Sapiens is of No Importance

And it may be that we have no nature
That he could have taken upon him.
Plato of course discussed it.
Deborah sitting under a tree
In a time of matriarchy:
Blessed be thou among women,
Blessed be the hand, the hammer,
Blessed the tent-peg as it drove through Sisera,
Blessed the connection between two interiors,
Blessed the wire between the switch and the bulb.
Not for the mind of Jael but for her hand
Not for the hand but for the hammer
Not for the hammer but for the tent-peg
Not for the peg but for Sisera dead
Not for Sisera dead but for his army routed
Not for that but the momentary ease under a tree
Not for that but for the tree itself
Not for the tree but the sand blowing by it.
If there was any nature it was in that.

The Man with a Family

In at the womb and out at the eyes.
There was no pardon for the children he had committed,
Twelve of them sitting round the table eating their porridge.
'How many roses have you broken off my stem
In the illusion that you were doing the gardening?'

In at the womb and out at the mouth.
The first word was fuck but there were a great many after it.
'It is odd that the exercise of seeking resemblance
Should end with such great distances between us.'

In at the womb and finally out of the ears
If we may suppose a spiritual substance to seek egress that way.
'I think it may, it does not know whether it is going or coming;
There is a certain confusion which is best expressed that way.'

Orpheus

The inside and the outside of the body;
These are the two minds that I am in.

If I seek to put you in mind of me
I assure you that nothing is further from my mind
Than that you should concern yourself with my exterior.

If on the other hand I put myself in mind of you
It is rather that you put yourself in my mind
And it is as a figure passing, stripped to the skin.

Yet you must be supposed to be also you,
A figure to whom the epidermis is indifferent
Or at best a superficial and tingling dress.

A group of naked figures with Orpheus playing
But succeeding in attracting only the animals
I take to be a representation of the mind.

Metamorphoses

I.

Actaeon was a foolish hind
To run from what he had not seen.

He was a hunter, and had called
An end to slaughter for that day

And laid his weapons by a well.
Diana knew the man he was

But took her kirtle from her waist.
She gave her arrows to her maids

Then dropped her short and flimsy dress.
There was some muscle on the girl.

I think she knew the hunt was up
But set the hounds upon the man

To show her bitter virgin spite.
There was some blood but not her own.

Actaeon sped, his friends hallo'ed,
The forest rang but not with tears.

His favourite whippet bit his flank:
His friends hallo'ed him to the kill

Which they were sure he would enjoy.
Diana by the fountain still

Shuddered like the water on her flesh
And after that there came the night.

II.

– Or else he was a rutting stag
Turned to a man because he saw

Diana bathing at the pool
– As you might turn a foreskin back.

III.

Pygmalion was an artful man;
Sculpsit and pinxit were his trade.

He would not have a woman in
The confines of his silky bed;

The ones he knew were troublesome.
Still, he admired the female form

And cut another in that shape
But it was marble, rather hard.

He laid it down upon his bed
And drew a purple coverlet

Across its shapely breasts and legs.
However, it did not respond.

He got it up and gave it clothes
And brought it several sorts of toys.

It did not speak a single word
So in despair he said his prayers.

He did not even dare to say
'This marble' or 'this ivory';

He merely said he'd like a girl
Resembling one he'd made himself.

After his prayers the boy went home
And got back to his kissing game.

To his surprise the girl grew warm;
He slobbered and she slobbered back

– This is that famous mutual flame.
The worst of all was yet to come.

Although he often wished her back
In silent marble, good and cold

The bitch retained her human heat,
The conquest of a stone by art.

May Venus keep me from all hope
And let me turn my love to stone.

IV.

O will you take a fluttering swan
Eurotas, on your plashy banks?

Where the dissimulating bird
Fled from a Venus he had coaxed

Into an eagle with a beak.
Eurotas showed beneath her waves

The rippling image of a girl.
She rose to take the frightened bird

And struggled with him to the bank.
It was the bird came out on top.

Its wings concealed the thing it did
But showed the fluttering legs and hands.

The bird became a stable thing:
There are such dangers for a girl.

Europa felt a sighing bull
Beside her, as she gathered flowers.

It was a gentle, milk-white beast
And tried to graze upon her hair.

She patted and embraced its neck;
Its breath grew deeper as she stroked.

At last she climbed upon his back,
One hand upon a stubby horn.

Over his broad and shaggy cloth
The creature felt the gentle limbs

And in a trice he was away.
Europa held the swimming beast;

She looked at the receding shore
And clutched her garments from the wind.

v.

When Virgo crosses with the Ram
Expect a rain of falling stars,

A spilling cornucopia
Betokening plenty, but no peace,

A Danae in her open boat.
The eleemosynary shower

That fell, can now get up again
And it is Easter in the world.

The first age was the age of gold;
The age of iron is our own.

vi.

The day, the year, the century,
The glacial winter, and the spring

And then the naked summer brings
The rutting stag to the church door.

But first the Phaeton from the crown
Of heavens descends into the waves.

There was no reason in his course
And on his way he burnt the world

And when you visited the shades
Did you see my Eurydice,

Christ, on that terrifying day?
I sit beneath the pulpit for

The bitter, abnegated hour.
I have no notion what you did.

In manus tuas. Afterwards.
Except you walked three days in hell.

Was there numb kindness in the shades?
Who is that nacreous figure there

The empty sunlight falls upon
Although there is no light to fall?

Will she resume the upper light?
And when you come to Thomas in

The confines of his doubting room
Was she left in an orange-grove?

There was a garden. Calvary.
And Adam fell where you got up.

But was the resurrected flesh
Less tempted than the flesh of Eve?

The naked figure in the grove
Diana's or the risen Christ's?

Her altar or the flesh we eat?
The world is uncreated by

The death of him that made the world.
By the slain lamb there trots the fawn.

VII.

Here are two stories of old men:
The virtuous Boaz is the first.

He lay upon the threshing floor
And dreamed of Ruth, who soon came in

And while in sleep he saw the fields
Where she had stooped to gather corn

She gently lifted, in the dark,
The rug that hid his bony toes.

It was a rather pleasant dream.
Benign and virtuous to himself

He wished he could be warm like Ruth.
And there she was. But he was scared.

He sent her home and merely bit
The aged spit upon his beard

And did it honestly next day.
As he was rich the world approved.

The second story is about
Two men whose desiccated years

Were sheltered in the splendid house
Of Joachim, a juicy lord.

They earned their keep by being just
But saw Susanna every day.

She was a soft and tender bit.
They noticed when she took her bath

And both devised a pleasant plan
To help her with the soap and rinse.

They waited in the garden where
She took it when the sun was hot.

Unhappily it warmed them too
And made them lie to get their way.

Then they were frightened, and resumed
Their great pretence of being just.

Less fortunate than Boaz, they
Could only hope to have her killed

But even this did not come off
And Daniel had them cut in two.

VIII.

Which otherwise might have been born.
They carried in a bloody tray

This unripe apple plucked within
The forest of the uterus.

This one at least will not arrive
At ages suitable for tears.

Within this forest everything
Begins. Although I may not say

Eurydice walks with her tears
It is the grove where they began.

It is the grove where I walked out,
Blind as upon my latest days.

I had a kind of folded life.
The butterfly with its wet wings

Has twice the power I had to fly.
And how then to the garden where

The loaded Tree of Knowledge stood?
Deceptively completed man

Beside a woman as complete?
No expectation in his eyes

His member like a falling leaf;
The fronded entrance to Eve's cave

Admitting no posterity.
The shining apples had no life.

Then how could Adam come to find
A tree more naked than himself,

Excoriate of leaves and fruit
And he himself nailed to the boughs?

Some serpent must have let him hope,
Which his glazed body could not do

Without hortation from a flesh
He had forgotten was his own.

Some spasm must have found its end
And broken his tumescent heart.

Eve must have let her children out
From her forced womb, to right and left.

But first, within, the spinning wave
Of sperm had sent its foam-flake out

To meet the southward-seeping egg
And this encounter did not hear

Either the paradisal speech
Exchanged when congress was agreed

Or the reared serpent's good advice
So soft that it became a hiss.

It needed Cain and Abel too,
The brothers Murder and Incite

And Noah with his upturned eyes,
Lifting his skirts out of the wet

And Abraham in fear of God,
Getting his holy cutlass out.

The sober, patriarchal life
In which the richest was the best

And now the surgeon with his smile
And sister's deferential cough.

IX.

The metamorphosis of all.
Or he was nothing but a child

Magi attended for the star
And shepherds for their singing ears.

Funny how he became a Mass,
To eat his body, when he died,

The first essay of carpentry
Building an ark for the whole world

As you might nail a coffin up.
The golden age began anew;

What had been first became the last.
Declension to the age of iron

Was unimportant after all.
And yet there must remain a doubt.

The giants piling up the sky,
Pelion on Ossa, also rose

And what will rise must also fall.
We know it by experience.

It is the waning of the year.
A death in spring-time is the best.

Stanza

Every year blackthorn and daffodil
Are noticed by those who imagine they are renewed
When the year is. But they grow old,
The renewal of hope is vain: it is their grandchildren
Who come laughing along the road, picking the cowslips.

An Essay on God and Man

I know nothing of it. The human race,
The individual, it is fashionable to say.
But what is that, a pronoun?
'Develop the personality
To the fullest extent.' That is a lark
More visible to those who believe their own words
Than to those who want to recall them
The moment they have been uttered
Because they have failed even to trace in the air
Something they had been about to say.
There are, as I see it, creatures with arms and legs
And the variable expression.
Brickbats, temples, words, the sculpsit and pinxit.
There is the night of each mind,
Like a squalid family snoring behind a blanket.
There is something there, you can hardly see it by candle-light.
Love? This monster is supposed to be linked with the person,
But again, I do not know.
It is a fine trick to tie love to the penis
Like the cracked fakirs who put a skewer through it.
'Marriage is for the procreation of children
And the prevention of fornication.'
The former a thing
Which has no need of individual consciousness,
The latter a piece of hygiene,
The mere removal of a possible public nuisance.
'Hallowing the instincts' and that stuff
A post-Darwinian invention in bad prose.
There are, really, only the things you notice,
With, as a matter of faith, those you do not.
But to erect this group of impressions
Into something you call the person
Is a gratuitous verbal trickery
Like many others which keep the world going.
A tree does not talk of developing itself;
If there is something in the way, it grows crooked.
And so may you. A child out of the womb
Has to be nappied, wiped, and educated
But this is something you do to him

As you might wash down your car and tinker with it.
It has nothing to do with the miracle of personality
Which is a subjective disease you first start admiring in yourself
Then pretend we are all growing happily together
As if flowering were not a matter of choking off others.
What you see is what you get.
Your share being different it is certain that you will not
Understand anyone else. What you can observe
Is the accuracy of others' responses, and classify them accordingly.
And if you believe in the Lord God
Jeering over this multitude and controlling their devices
You will not be tempted to anything but the adjustments
Your machine is capable of in its reaction with others.
Lenin remarked
That God was a complex of ideas
Born out of the subjection of man to nature
– And thought he had found him out.
But I cheerfully accept this definition
As corresponding, more than most, to a reality.

The Consequence

I.
There is no more to say than No
And Nothing is my farthest end.
A man has pity for his friend
But I am only glad to go.
Now therefore let the handsome crow
Pick out the eyes I would not lend.

II.
We feed on death for half our lives
But vomit when we let it in.
The final pallor of the skin
Betokens that the patient thrives.
How earnestly the swimmer dives!
How eager his returning fin!

III.
Old age protects itself with hope
And leans to suck the kiss of youth.

How kindly Boaz took to Ruth!
The lion with the antelope.
And what delighted fingers grope
In cradles to forget the truth!

IV.
But there is twilight and the rose
And other such ephemera.
The crocus and Proserpina
Distract us to a brief repose.
And I, who have a polished heart,
Harder than any sympathy
But excellent for lechery
Or any sanctimonious part
For ever leave the truth alone;
It crunches time up like a stone
While love, the centre of the mind
Nibbles the flesh from head to feet.
The dusty streets of Sodom find
Two constables upon the beat.

V.
Plato, whom reason ate like sex,
Preferred the form before the thing.
But what contentment did that bring?
Whom did that ever unperplex?
Meanwhile incessant number pecks
At form, until the scaffolding
Of all our thoughts is down, to fling
The gates of chaos on our necks.
Judas went out and hanged himself
And so should I, for I am he.
There is no Adam to set free.

VI.
The forest of a long intent
Has tracks where I may lose my way
Nor was the place I am today
Intended by the way I went.
The night has only disarray;
It does not see what day mistook.

What was it that the nightmare shook?
Although I heard the drum today
The same occasions day by day
Provide me with identity.
I do what the occasions say
For nothing never is without
The thing it wants, and for its play
A futile gesture is the best.

Catullus

Catullus walked in the Campus Martius.
He had seen all he needed to see,
Lain on his bed at noon, and got up to his whore.
His heart had been driven out of his side
By a young bitch – well, she was beautiful,
Even, while the illusion was with him, tender.
She had resolved herself into splayed legs
And lubricity in the most popular places.
He had seen Caesar who – had he not been, once,
The drunken pathic of the King of Bithynia? –
Returning in triumph from the western isles:
Nothing was too good for this unique emperor.
Against these fortunes he had nothing to offer
– Possibly the remains of his indignation,
A few verses that would outlive the century.
His mind was a clear lake in which he had swum:
There was nothing but to await a new cloud.
We have seen it. But Catullus did not;
He had already hovered his thirty years
On the edge of the Mediterranean basin.
The other, rising like a whirlwind in a remote province,
Was of a character he would have ignored.
And yet the body burnt out by lechery,
Turning to its tomb, was awaiting this,
Forerunning as surely as John the Baptist
An impossible love pincered from a human form.

VALEDICTION
Catullus my friend across twenty centuries,
Anxious to complete your lechery before Christ came.

In Preparation for an Epitaph

Letters have been the passion of my life
Habit the habit and affairs the bane:
If by passion you mean a continuous attention
Intermitted for everything more important
And by a bane what only partially kills
That is it. Now I am nearly fifty
It is the habit which shrouds me as I go down to death
(For in my sense the bane is working at last).
It is only the tombstone that I shall regret
For which I might have written a noble inscription.

Words

I have noticed that words are not understood.
Where the dappled fawns walk in the sunlight
In contrast with their sisters dark against the sky-line
The beeches crack.

My Life and Times

I would not waste this paper for
(I hope) a merely personal bore
But write about the singular
Because 'I am' may read 'We are.'
So damn the individual touch
Of which the critics make so much;
Remember that the human race
Grins more or less in every face.

My mind unfocussed like my eyes,
When young I showed, not felt, surprise.
Perhaps. But what comes from the womb
Is all that goes into the tomb
Or more than all. And what we mean
Or may imagine in between
Is trivial by comparison.
It is the gloss that we put on.

My elders recognised my shape.
Thereafter there was no escape
For parents do the best they can
To capture us and make us Man.
So I became subjective too
And what was hopeful now is true.

As my especial mode of thought
Was finding where I had not sought,
When Love at last possessed my mind
It was exactly of that kind.
There was no exercise of will;
It came, I saw it and stood still.
It was a blaze and I was dark.
The grief that scorched me left the mark.

No money and much time to spend.
I walked the streets for hours on end
Then lay upon my iron bed.
Some have their youth. This was instead.

What mattered when I left this shore
And found the classic world of war?
I understood the natural hate
Of man and cruelty of state
And the Schutz Staffel was to me
The natural heart of Germany.

War happened like a second birth
Upon an even blinder earth:
Some happy to increase the rate
At which they drink and fornicate
But exile and anxiety
For others. This included me.
From this excitement then I come
To settle soberly at home
And, blindly occupied with work,
I live completely in the dark.
For I have reached that slippery place
Where Nisus fell upon his face
While his young friend ran on. The truth

Took over from the hopes of youth.
Rather, I saw the limits of
Even the promises of love.
This moment comes, early or late.
Rather, you slide into a state
In which the heart is running on
Perhaps, but expectation's gone.
For the first part of life we move
To get to where we came from – love.
Then time is moving and we stand.
Something descends and is at hand.
There are innumerable ways
Of marking the *nel mezzo* phase
But all men understand that breath
Grows shorter long before our death.
So I, improvident, looked round
And saw that I was losing ground
And that it did not matter for
To win would also be a bore.
I could say, like some wily man
I had thought out a clever plan.
In fact, it worked the other way;
I did what offered day by day.
Small children climbed upon my face
Or ran in front to set the pace.
The only secret of 'I go'
Is following what you do not know.
I burrow in an office where
There is no purpose in despair.
This is, indeed, the last descent.
But how await the sure event?
For time will wave his arms about
Until he gives his final shout.

The Nature of Man

It is the nature of man that puzzles me
As I walk from Saint James's Square to Charing Cross;
The polite mechanicals are going home,
I understand their condition and their loss.

Ape-like in that their box of wires
Is shut behind a face of human resemblance,
They favour a comic hat between their ears
And their monkey's tube is tucked inside their pants.

Language which is all our lies has us on a skewer,
Inept, weak, the grinning devil of comprehension; but sleep
Knows us for plants or undiscovered worlds;
If we have reasons, they lie deep.

A Letter to John Donne

> *Note: On 27 July, 1617, Donne preached at the parish church at Sevenoaks, of which he was rector, and was entertained at Knole, then the country residence of Richard Sackville, third Earl of Dorset.*

I understand you well enough, John Donne
First, that you were a man of ability
Eaten by lust and by the love of God
Then, that you crossed the Sevenoaks High Street
As rector of Saint Nicholas:
I am of that parish.

To be a man of ability is not much
You may see them on the Sevenoaks platform any day
Eager men with despatch cases
Whom ambition drives as they drive the machine
Whom the certainty of meticulous operation
Pleasures as a morbid sex a heart of stone.

That you could have spent your time in the corruption of courts
As these in that of cities, gives you no place among us:
Ability is not even the game of a fool
But the click of a computer operating in a waste

Your cleverness is dismissed from this suit
Bring out your genitals and your theology.

What makes you familiar is this dual obsession;
Lust is not what the rutting stag knows
It is to take Eve's apple and to lose
The stag's paradisal look:
The love of God comes readily
To those who have most need.

You brought body and soul to this church
Walking there through the park alive with deer
But now what animal has climbed into your pulpit?
One whose pretension is that the fear
Of God has heated him into a spirit
An evaporated man no physical ill can hurt.

Well might you hesitate at the Latin gate
Seeing such apes denying the church of God:
I am grateful particularly that you were not a saint
But extravagant whether in bed or in your shroud.
You would understand that in the presence of folly
I am not sanctified but angry.

Come down and speak to the men of ability
On the Sevenoaks platform and tell them
That at your Saint Nicholas the faith
Is not exclusive in the fools it chooses
That the vain, the ambitious and the highly sexed
Are the natural prey of the incarnate Christ.

A and B

A.
I was in the lane and saw the car pass.
The white face of the girl showed through the windscreen,
Beside her a youth with a tight grip on the wheel.
B.
There was a blue Anglia; I remember.

A.
I caught the girl's eyes as she passed;
They were in deepest contentment.
She communicated in perfect freedom to me
The candour with which she would undress when they reached
    the wood.
It was a point that had been troubling the boy.
B.
And what has their pleasure to do with us?
A.
You think a philosopher should stick to his port.
That is not my opinion.
What is enacted in these hills
Is a sacrifice as any propounded
Under the shadow of the Giant of Cerne
And sacrifice is not for the actors.
B.
What nonsense is this about a sacrifice?
This is what two people did, and that is all.
A.
What they did in a flurry of consciousness,
Their hands upon one another's sides,
Was trivial enough. But what were their intentions?
Some hope perhaps of giving or taking pleasure.
B.
I should think they might have been partially successful.
A.
I met an old man on a tall horse
He had ridden for thirty years. It was his intention
When he had seen the last of it, to bury it
Out in that field beside his dead mare.
Do you think he had planned that harmony?
Did not a spirit seize him by the throat
And tell him what to do: there, under the old church
Rising there on that mound above the groin?
B.
I am afraid, A, you are not a philosopher.
You are merely an inconsiderate fool who loves his country
At the very moment when love has become vain.

A.
See there where a party of picnickers
Trace their way over the springy turf
And the world proceeds without understanding.
Perhaps all will be well.

Good-Day, Citizen

My life is given over to follies
More than I can exaggerate:
If I told you half you would imagine
That I am a very respectable person.

First, there is the folly of earning money
In order to have what is called independence:
You can admire that quality if you will,
I know what it is and do not admire it.

Secondly, there is the folly of spending it wisely,
So much for insurance, so much for the house,
Suitable provision for the children's education
Which for the most part they would rather not have.

Thirdly there would be, if that were not in fact all,
The supervening graces of domestic virtue
Everything paid up, honest as the day
But I am nearest to my own language in sleep.

At First

Nothing that is said or done
Can equal in the end
The first apprehension of love.
And so it is at last.
Speak, God, to the encumbered
Servant I am. It will be news
If you tell me I am saved.

Eros

One must be blind if there shall be love.
The grey-haired woman running with a small child
Feeds on a hope she can no longer enjoy:
The lunacy makes her straggling hair wild.
I expect no hope but what comes from without
If there were not a blind god I should be in doubt.

Of two walking in arms along the pavement
– There are her buttocks through her summer frock –
One at least will repent.
It is the one that understands now
The passion of the god; whom contemplation
Drives to a madness that should be doing.

Oh, I have stood appalled before beauty
With no speech but gratitude; who will not betray that?
Understanding was too far in my heart:
None could make sense of me. Is not
That the delirious impotence of youth
For those who later are to take refuge in truth?

Now I seek daily for my own blindness
In the assertion reason cannot mitigate
And now an impotent old man comes running:
It is him I go to meet.
Will you not cut me one tress for tenderness,
Eros, because I acknowledge the blind?

Act Munday

(*See Anthony a Wood, July 11, 1692*)

A body that was stubbornly dead
They carried out and brought him to All Hallows,
Under the upper window in the north churchyard.
Young men carried him, maids at his funeral
Extended a white sheet over his stiff corpse,
Reluctant, as they might be, to let him depart.

An Old Man

Old man with white hair falling
Over your eyes, my experience
Will be very ripe when I am like you.
You could stand on one leg and sing,
Having little of what is called sense
– Little also left of your senses it is true.

Your eyes decayed, you cannot see the sparrow
Unless he perches on top of your spade
More of a flutter than a seen thing;
You cannot smell the invisible rose
Only your body odours and the general autumn,
The acrid smoke of the bonfire that makes you spit.

In and out of the trees you go to die in the jungle
Scratching among the leaves you find no grave.
It is a worm you turn up
There is no reed you do not mistake for Syrinx.
These are unsuitable favours for you to crave
But you have no objection to being a fool.

The ambition not to be one is still too strong for me;
It is this which makes you wiser than I
But your alarmed features declare
That you have not altogether found peace.
Are you still aware of the passing time?
Your mouth has failed but your eyes try to remember.

While your amnesia is only partial
You grope round reality like a mathematician:
There are degrees of folly.
It is not odd to find the world unintelligible
So, until merciful death comes
Creep round your garden, all the town protects you.

The Thrush

You do not see your speckled breast and bright eye;
What you eat is what interests you. I do not eat
You but I am interested and have the name beauty
For your feathered and energetic stand and sharp beak.

This is what it is to be the image of God:
I am it because I reflect your image,
Loving without eating. But eating
Is the end of loving. No wonder if I am confused.

And this young beauty is aware of herself
From shoulder to shank she is for discovery
By herself as well as by the hungry who would eat her.
Her mind is out of the order of nature.

It is puzzling that the form of natural good
Is a little different from the specifically human.
Those who out of congress invented lechery
Were the first inventors of man and woman.

Adam and Eve

They must be shown as about to taste of the tree.
If they had already done so they would be like us;
If they were not about to do so they would be
Not our first parents but monsters.

You must show that they were the first who contrived
An act which has since become common,
With head held high when it is conceived
And, when it is repented of, dangling.

There must be not one Adam but two,
The second nailed upon the tree:
He came down in order to go up
Although he hangs so limply.

The first Adam, you will recall, gave birth
To a woman out of his side;
For the second the process was reversed
And that one was without pride.

Easter

One good crucifixion and he rose from the dead
He knew better than to wait for age
To nibble his intellect
And depress his love.

Out in the desert the sun beats and the cactus
Prickles more fiercely than any in his wilderness
And his forty days
Were merely monastic.

What he did on the cross was no more
Than others have done for less reason
And the resurrection you could take for granted.

What is astonishing is that he came here at all
Where no one ever came voluntarily before.

Nuptials

The clever ape with the hyaena laugh
Wishes to obscure the image of man.
His teeth walk out of him, he leans back in his chair
And reason vibrates in him like a humming-top.

Behind closed doors he laughs his trousers off,
Advances with wide hands upon his prey,
Who at one time thought that a superlative love
Must lurk in a character so coaxed and combed.

The complications of his logic-board
Are no help to his tender victim;
Nothing can be said and the brilliant mind
Falls on her like a heap of scaffolding.

By the Lift Gate

Well I can understand your contraction
The lines by your eyes and your pointed nose:
You pull your coat about you (but I can guess)
Advancing one foot with suspended toes.

The melancholy at the approach of winter
Is not for the season but the summer lost,
Your juices retracted, but not yet gone
The moment, you would probably say, passed.

But whether you reached for that moment
And so fell headlong into the abyss
Or waited on the brink, all is one in the end:
You are approaching forty and no peace.

I have hunted your eyes like weasels among the ferns:
Who can say when there is an end of hope
Or what peace there would have been in satisfaction?
Close the lift gate and go up on the end of a rope.

Great Down

With the great book of nature open upon your knees
You sit like a comptometer on the hill-side,
Reckoning the church-spires. Is what the machine
Records a proper object of pride?
Is it more than the animal can scent?
Is there also human consent?

The naked Bororo divides his village
And without this geometry loses his faith:
Others have trudged in the course of the sun.
Mechanical compulsions are not of this age.
The best rule is that you should seek to please;
Go down on your back or on your knees.

How were you taught when young to be you?
You had not been invented before, there was no pattern.

Your parents invented you as you grew;
They gave you a name and their love and you learned
That there was no alternative to being a person,
Never suspecting the sense of that tradition.

You will deny that you were born to ask
That your few feet of flesh should have hope.
Proud fool! You think you are degraded by asking
And yet, of all the mind's movements, this is the top:
First, for what I may give you in your womb,
And then, for what you will find for yourself in the tomb.

A Young Woman

You straddle in the street like Atalanta.
You were somebody's daughter not long ago,
Now mother to this brood.
You extend one hand to a straw-haired child;
Another trips over your long back leg
As you run laughing towards a third.

There is a cave in your athletic belly
From which these made their way to the fragrant world.
Now they are like petals but the lines gather
Already about your eyes;
The flesh you took into your bridal bed
Is already such that the boys no longer whistle.

Soon you will understand that hope
Which you at present pursue
Has to be carried like water in a cup.
At last you will hold it so,
The race having turned to mere knowledge
And you by the fire or fingering the turned-down sheet.

Grandmother

Grandmother wheeling a perambulator
With outstretched arms and senescent leer,
What reason for hope have you here?
Shame on the body at fourscore!

Only Christ can have mercy on you now;
You can look for none from Venus or Lucina.
The boy's stout finger admonishes you
What a danger to women he intends to be.

Turn up the pram and let him tumble upon
The flat silk front that covers your dugs.
You are glad to feel the strength of his legs;
He is harmless in your lap as others were not.

Once you gave your body to the poor.
That will sustain you now more than any prudence.
Now you may give it to this young impotent
As he laughs and kicks but you know more.

Grandmother you may perambulate
With broken spokes and distorted frame;
You are cheerful and it may be half crazed
Not for what you have but for what you gave.

Loquitur Senex

I return to the horror of truth
After a life of business:
I was happy to be employed
But now my hunger is extreme.

The swans drift by and the bridge
Is pendulous over the profound stream:
The water is habitable by the mind
And the stationary fish are swimming against it.

Where were the fish when I,
Flurried by consultation,

Laboured to distinguish myself
In vanity and discursive reason?

Now, with the fish, nose pressed
Against reality,
I look through the watery glass
At weeds standing on stone.

The age is lost that had
Laughter hidden under the hand
But in the peace that remains
There is still what lives in the eye.

Gracious God, when the tension gives
And I am swept below the weir
Do as Berkeley says
Hold this world in your mind.

Things Seen

When the bomb has fallen
And the land is scored
With burns over its once delicious green
Time will be erased from these walls
And not even the written word
Call back things seen.

Look your fill while you may,
Burying your face in woods as among the dew
And turn home at nightfall
Where the children's voices promise no posterity
Or as much as a cat where they grew
And the only certainty is that night will fall.

The Nature-Lover

Where the hare with her slight thoughts
Passes and the badger leaves his bones
My eyes fill with them and the fields,
But this boy with the gun has the right idea:
It is by killing that we join in their fun.

The Lion Man

It is a mud-cracked world. A scaly sun
Has frowned on it since day began.
Picking them from the floor Imo has thrown
Komo's arrows out of the house.
I do not know what it means; it is an insult.

Imo has a niece.
One day when this child
Walks into the scrub to leave her turd out of sight
The women release the lion man, I suppose by a word.
There is nothing more to this story: a few entrails,
A few bones, a few rags left in the jungle.
Imo should not have thrown those arrows out of the house.

The Temple

Who are they talking to in the big temple?
If there were a reply it would be a conversation:
It is because there is none that they are fascinated.
What does not reply is the answer to prayer.

In Memoriam Cecil de Vall

late garrison chaplain, Barrackpore

You can count me as one who has hated
Out of spoiled love rather than malice.
Let me lie now between tufts of heather,
My head in the grass.

The sky is too high, I prefer to be far under it
The road is happily distant.
No angel shall catch me here, nor tourist
Abase me with his talk.

Out from this patch of dust the flat plain
Extends like Asia under a blue sky.
It is no misanthropy that binds me here
But recognition of my own failure.

I ask no better than that
The long convolvulus shall grow over me
And prickling gorse
Keep the children away.

Soon the fallen flesh will begin to crawl
Making off in the worm's belly
Into the undergrowth, and the polished flies
Will riddle me like hat-pins.

I bid their rising lives welcome because
It is better to be many than one;
The mirrors of blue-bottle and worm
May reflect to more purpose than I.

Curl my fin where the shark
Lurches in the blue Mediterranean;
Open my wizened eye
Like a lizard under a tropical leaf.

As I bite the dust of this flat land
For the last time, with dissolving chaps,

Keep me free from all such reflection
Lest the mind dazzle as it goes out.

I do not wish to recognise Christ
As I enter the shades.
What other company could I have
In darkness of my own choosing?

Perhaps it is no more than a recollection
– The banks of a river,
The heavy vegetation wet with the monsoon,
My friend on the verandah?

He brought out the long whiskies and proved
That God hated nothing that He had made:
At no time did I take at his hands
Any but his own hospitality.

Fill my mouth with sand, let the passer's boot
Unwittingly fold my skull.
I have resigned the pretensions
Of the individual will.

From the darkened shores of the river
The dogs howled;
I was alone with the famished and the dead.
Whatever stirred in those shadows was not God.

Eclogue

CORYDON, DAPHNIS
Put the buggers under the wall.
No one will notice that you have strangled the bastards.
Thus Corydon, regardful of his flock.
Daphnis took a bunch of *parfum chèvre*
In his great mit and, having adjusted his jock-strap,
Set out to dazzle or woo the incomparable Chloe.
I suppose she was lying on her back
With her legs wide open, pretending to snore.
At any rate Daphnis made short work of her.
Back with his mates, Corydon took up the pipe:

All things were made for the violent and the greedy.
Thank you, Pan, for your inclination towards us.

STREPHON, DORINDA
STREPHON: So, Dorinda, you will not take my garland
Although I am an educated shepherd;
I pipe all day but you cannot hear me.
DORINDA: Too apt a replica of human life
Is apt to distress those for whom it is intended.
STREPHON: You know a trick better than distress;
You sit all day with your knees hunched,
Your mind concentrated on counting your lambs.
If you took our country pleasures
You might suddenly become endowed with understanding.
DORINDA: That is a fantasy of the adolescent
And really only a pun on carnal knowledge.
The shepherd who seeks to move me with his pipe
Does not thereby acquire a right to my conversation.
STREPHON: But if the understanding is not carnal
It is no more than your tallies without your sheep.
DORINDA: Do not press me to accept that argument.
I will bathe myself in the clear stream
But do not join me, Strephon.

DORINDA, DAPHNIS, CORYDON
DAPHNIS: Hey, Corry, that tart is taking her clothes off.
CORYDON: Leave her; she don't need no help from you.
DAPHNIS: Watch me. Daphnis is the boy for this.
DORINDA: Daphnis, you are deceived by your own name.
DAPHNIS: I never heard a tart who spoke like that before.
DORINDA: Which of your two tongues is the more eloquent
I have, I assure you, not the slightest doubt.
Even with a voice of full-throated melody
It is hard enough to say what is being expressed,
A fortiori with a tongue which merely licks.
DAPHNIS: Lie down over there and I will show you.
If Strephon can't manage you well then I can.
DORINDA: It is not in the management but in what is managed
Or rather in whether what is distinguished from who
That the problem lies
And if that is the limit of your invention

You will really get us no nearer a solution.
Corydon, taking his pipe, induced this song:
Charm without thinking, calf-deep in the splashing water
Under the green shadow that makes your flesh a thought.

DAPHNIS, STREPHON
DAPHNIS: Shepherds without identity is a good lark
– Dorinda and me copulating like flies.
To be nothing but an objective buzz!
STREPHON: For you that is a comprehensible ambition
Because you are not aware that being an object
Is different in kind from observing what is.
Even the pleasure you took with Chloe,
Vigorous and unreflective though it was,
Did not succeed in reaching annihilation
Nor can you forget her foul breath
Or the way her teeth met you.
DAPHNIS: Chloe was all right though she stank a bit
But what I should like is to get Dorinda
When she has stopped being a naiad.
STREPHON: Corydon's song was meant to warn you against that
As much as to silence Dorinda.
It was only an echo from the philosophers
Came from her lips and reverberated through the grotto
And philosophy is harmless enough.
But for you to suppose you could achieve brutality
And become like a May-bug driven against a pane
By uniting yourself with one so rational
Is to misunderstand the nature of love.

DAPHNIS, STREPHON, DORINDA
DORINDA: Indeed it is the nature of love which is in question
But why either of you should think he can be united
Merely by favour of a ridiculous pipe
With someone conceived of as an entity
Of a different kind, is more than I can say.
STREPHON: Dorinda, you are a monster of vanity.
You understand well enough that the problem
Is not the penetration of your superb self
But how we come to be talking of it.
If you in fact had been that slight figure,

More gracious than I can say, among the rushes
I need have been no more than my eyes.
It was in that moment Corydon made his song.
That was no sooner ended, however, than this lout
Daphnis, for ever with his mind on the bacon,
Comes up with his unremunerative plans for action
And you quickly lay claim to an identity
Which means you must not be touched.

DAPHNIS, STREPHON, DORINDA, CORYDON
CORYDON: My verse also was a deception.
It is time we came to the sheep-shearing.
Here, Daphnis, take hold of this crook.
Go and collect the flock from the long meadow.
Strephon, you get the antiseptic shears
And grind them on the stone behind the dairy.
I will look after Dorinda.

DORINDA, CORYDON
CORYDON: Put on your clothes and come and eat a posset
Of curds and whey under the great oak.
Perhaps you would care to be my secretary;
I need a girl with brains to count my sheep.
DORINDA: Well, that would certainly be better than love;
I am rather fed up with being admired.
I should like instead to be useful.
CORYDON: You could be doubly so if you came with me.
I have employment enough for your intelligence
And at night, when we have counted our money,
We will play at natural objects.
DORINDA: I cannot too much praise your invention.
Midas was embarrassed by his golden touch
But you turn gold to nature.
CORYDON: So that is fixed?
DORINDA: I will accept you if you make it legal.

DAPHNIS, STREPHON, CORYDON, DORINDA
DAPHNIS AND STREPHON: Everything is ready for the
    sheep-shearing.
DORINDA: Boys, I shall enjoy watching you work.

No Title

I will tell you the story of my success:
I had lived in great obscurity before,
The room was literally dark, I came and went
As a person without mystery, gifted with reason.
It was a hell and an obscure one,
But the more specious hell I live in now
Full of light and colours, and predestination
Moving my arms like windmills and my legs like a treadmill.
My nature is not what I am
But what these manipulations appear to be.
It is not the world that is reflected in my eye
But the dark interior of my face.
There are two kinds of being, recognition
Making the larger out of the dust
Which composed the meaner and more exact person.
It is as if I had become somebody else
Not by becoming another person but by becoming
Some of the things one person may seem to another.
As if, by pretending, I had become a stone,
Not as something inert but a seen thing
Instead of a seeing thing, and the corruption
Which should wait to seize the body till death
Already begins to eat at my living carcase.

Being is not necessarily at one with person;
It is rare indeed for the conception
To fit in the body or even the manner of walking.
This person who conceives ideas
Carries a tangle drawn from all quarters
His own mind is unexpressed
It is the last of those that find voice.
This hair, these toes, and these excreta
Walk in the form of fashion, not their own.
The body is not more clad than the mind:
The bowler hat and the supporting stick
Give courage to the unadmitted nude.
It is this lie and this silence
Which comprise the excellence of the world.
I have that excellence now;
It is certainly a splendid thing to be successful.

Thomas de Quincey

Thomas de Quincey lying on the hearth-rug
With a finished manuscript at his side,
His bare feet in slippers and, tied up with ribbon,
There was his mind.

Of course it was stupor that he wanted
But his mind would work.
He followed the eloquence whose end is silence
Into the dark.

The Theology of Fitness

This is what I call mind:
Your behind,
That patch of hair in front,
Your navel, your cunt,
Your nipples, your lips;
The hair in your arm-pits
(If a depilatory
Have rased that memory
The hair on your head
Will do instead).
Starting at the nape
I examine your shape;
It is intellectual
And accordingly small.
There is the line
As I descend your spine
To your two legs
Split like a clothes peg.
Quelle heureuse pensée!
You will probably say
If I want a ewe to tup
I should start higher up
And, for example, surprise
Your intellect in your eyes.
Wishing merely to understand,
Lady, I kiss your hand.

Consider, since that is you
Who I am, who
Address these courtesies
And seek to please.
Shall I admit my mind
Starts in my behind
Or that my balls and hair
Give my verse its air?
(Less pleasant to dwell upon
I find, it is all one.)
This is my fund of wit
And cavity for shit.
Oh, there is much else
Still, when I see myself
I do not over-emphasise
The intelligence of my eyes.

So, when we resurrect
That which was once erect
(Although, in paradise
The suits are without flies)
Your spirit and your bum
Will certainly be one;
Every orifice
Will receive a kiss;
The lowly heart
Will trumpet out a fart;
There will be hosannas
From long bananas.

That being so
What shall we do now?

What a Piece of Work is Man

The man of quality is not quite what he was
In the days when that was a technical term
But there are, happily, a number of qualities
You can be a man of, and it is hard if there is not one
In which you can claim distinction.

Like speaks only to like, and without quality
Which you cannot communicate because you have it by blood
Or some subtler misfortune known as intelligence
There can be no speech.
It is by quality that you are not alone.
Those gathered around the bar, as they lift their beer-mugs
Tremble to break the enchantment of what is common:
It is so by the well or the dhobi-ghat
Or the club where charm may not exceed a pattern.
Pray do not address me in Japanese
In which language my hopes express themselves ill.
Yet what I have in common with the cat
Suffices for a very short conversation
Each time we meet.

Love is of opposites, they say: but the opposite
Is by way of being a philosophical refinement
And what wedges itself in the female slot
Though apposite enough, is hardly that.
If what goes on there is understanding
Then understanding is something different.
Do not imagine the body cannot lie;
What else have we for lying or for truth?
We talk by species and genus.
God who created us made himself understood
First in the thunder, then in the cloud and then in us.
I wish I did not hear him in the thunder.

How does it happen that the table leg
Has this curve in one age, that in another?
Or that the carved figures of men
Differ more than the men themselves?
Conception rules the art.
How then can one man speak to another?

Is it not the conception
Past any man's thinking, that is expressed
Even in the voice that seems to speak clearly?
And in the million voices that chatter together
Over this peninsula or that continent
A peculiar god looms

And what seems to be said between two people
Is only part of a complex conversation
Which they cannot hear and could not understand.
Yet it is only by taking part in that conversation
That they can give names to their own movements.
I lift my hand: there is a hand, certainly.
I touch your cheek: a hand touches a cheek.
In the name of what god? I have no name of my own.
Can I see my own movement except in conception?
What art has the heart, how does it understand
Its own beat?
The heart opened and the body chilled
Or the mind unneeded because the body is perfect.
The leaves of the jungle are parted. There comes out
One who moves like a deer.
And in the city the tapes record the prices,
Which is also a mode of understanding.

Words are not necessary between bodies.
O admirable attempt to forget to be human.
But you are clothed in words
Less of your own devising than your own body
And of which nothing can strip you but death.
Age and forgetfulness may leave you mumbling,
The words eating your toes or soft belly:
How are you speaking now?

A Girl

You speak of love, as if there were
Some certainty that it is here.
I see you coming and avert
My eyes lest they should do you hurt.
Your gentle limbs are confident
It is a woman that was meant
And yet, the very eyes you please
Destroy you with analyses.
It is not merely that my mind
Alas, is lecherous more than kind
And so distinguishes a part

It could not fairly call your heart,
Though I admit that, in the end,
The piston may destroy the friend.
My aching doubt is worse than that.
The human tasks that you are at
Neither begin nor end in you
Though in your mind you think they do.
With admiration you admire
What pulls you like a puppet wire.
How dare you claim a special you
Invented by the way you grew?
How can it be the words you use
Are really there for you to choose?
No mind, no error; but the grace
I worship in your holy face
Could hardly be without a mind.
How did you guess at human kind?
You walk by faith. If there is love
You see it pouring from above.

The Reckoning

My life dates from the day of my father's death
When I lay weeping and it was not for him.
Now I am to continue the degenerescence
Until I enter his dream.

There is nothing a drink cannot settle at forty
Or money at fifty, the cure of all is death.
But all lovers can remember a moment
When they were not alone.

From a Train

Two on a railway bank
They do not need their own thoughts
Their organs hanging on the verge.

The hanging gardens of Babylon
Flower in vast space between their legs
They crouch with great knees side by side.

Hands laced across the shoulders O
The light electrical touch of reason
O need they give each other names?

Go home at last to parents' eyes
The spirit unscaling as you go
Unlace those arms and be alone.

What you will not believe as you lie down
And call on God for the fornication you did not dare
Is that by chastity you have begun your age.

This loneliness will become your natural condition
When everything has been added and taken away
You will be left with a small grit which is yourself.

Amour Propre

Are there twenty-five
Fingers to one mind?
Are there seventy-three
An eye-lash and some teeth?
Does one skin make a whole
Remarkable soul?
Does anything prove
The mind is made of love?
Is it more in the bub
Than in the tunnelling grub?
Is the sword that makes a wife
Replaced by a knife?
So hard it is to know
What love should do.

Consequences

Why should I not allow myself to speak?
After his face changed and his mouth grew weak
I first understood mortality.
Then it took root in me
Now all I look upon
Turns to dissolution.

Numbers

I.
Now you have left that face I am perplexed
To find no one where I have loved best.
That is why, in the High Street, I stare
Wondering whether there is anyone anywhere.

II.
Nothing that is remembered is true
– And what precisely does that make of you?

III.
Please now leave indignation alone.
It is enough if you are a stone.
There are the mountains, the waving trees, and you
Flat on the open ground from which they grew.

IV.
If there were time it would be time to go
– It is the lack of it makes me rage so.
Yet you may say, laughter would do as well
Since for the eternal all things are possible.

V.
I said this man would fall and he fell.
With power dreams become terrible.
The power is nothing and the dream is all.

VI.
Let me escape the burning wheel of time.
There is no other purpose in rhyme

– As if a man could be identified
At least for his folly after he had died.

VII.
You come from sleep like a body from the womb
A moist wisp, and struggle into bloom.
There is an instant of delicacy, then
You strumpet unnoticed through a world of men.

VIII.
Lechery in age is not kind.
It is the last exercise of the mind.

IX.
Do not burn, my heart
– That would be to exaggerate your part.
It would not do for you to reduce to tears
One who has carried you for fifty years.

X.
If there were not air what would there be?
The voice passed my ear musically
Yet somehow I managed to be aware
Of what she was talking about – the air.
There were spirits in it, not least her own.
They are a substance immediately known
So there was no trouble about using the body
And that, for the moment, satisfied me completely.

XI.
Clifford says the mind is destroyed by work
And I agree my mind is destroyed by work.

XII.
Age, you have reached others before me.
They do not again expect to see me.
As they say good-bye they do not even have tears
Lest they seem to acknowledge their fears.

XIII.
They do not know whether they are going to rest
Or a long recession from what they have loved best.

The truth in those old eyes and in my own
Is all that was said in that conversation.

XIV.
He says good-bye from his wooden chair.
We go out and he is left there.
But which of us sees most vividly in the street
The boys and girls passing on featherweight feet?

XV.
I saw five hares playing in the snow.
That was only a winter ago
Yet they dance in my eyes and are as wild
As if I were old and had seen them as a child.

The Shortest Day

How can you tell whether a man is human?
Surely Christ must have mercy on the souls of animals
How else could I know who is my neighbour?

I met a man running across a plain
With taut cheeks and movements like an engine
There is need of mercy for me who encountered him.

Is it arms and legs, the long hands
The armoury of sex and the spoken word
Or what little the premature foetus is born with?

It cannot be only those I can speak to
It is those who are answerable to God
– May I be content not to identify them.

Badger my friend on the periphery of the city
The snow covers the time of the Incarnation
And I cannot understand the hard mind of God.

Christmas at the Greyhound

'All strangers now; there is nobody that I know.'
Draw near to the hearth; there is one nature of fire.

The Luxembourg

It must be admitted that they are historic,
These ladies – young ladies I mean – walking in the Luxembourg:
How else distinguished from Marie de Medici,
This girl bending over the edge of the *bassin*?
She is whatever she would be doing
Which she would because she comes from where she does –
Out of this *appartement* half way up the cliff of that building
With a childhood in this or that *ville de province* –
Not undetermined, resting in the hand of God
Who broods menacingly over all our fornications.

The Leopard and the Lynx

The lynx and the leopard stand
At the entrance of the forest
They paw and sniff.
Enter if you can
Pass their muzzles softly
If you would be safe.

Their eyes are on the ground
Dust rises out of it
As their soft pads strike.
What in their behaviour
Makes you invisible
As velvet in the night?

Go then, naked one,
Into the forest
Where the flat leaves breathe
Like a sleeper and
Fingers for all your dress
Cannot give security.

The leopard laughs like a drain
And the lynx too
Now you have crept by.
Why should they not be gay,

He or he, so
Patient till you would try?

Wander though you do
With all your skin on
Yet be not proud:
He or he, no longer demure,
The leopard or the lynx
Will eat you when you come out.

Two Shepherds

A: Now let us walk together, knowing
There is nothing to sing.
Winter and summer have been over us
More than enough times, and spring
Will not come unless we are envious,
Which we no longer are.
B: All the fleeces now are in one place,
Real or imagined the black faces
Have one thought. My ram
Climbs on the back of what is.
This is full of promise.

The Ragman

Well, it was wife or mother by
The cold fire.
The ragman at the door.
'He has come, in the night, I am alone
As he might think.'
A heavy tread
Comes down the stairs.
'Ragman, what are you?'
'I will force an entry.'
Two sides of the door.
The grandfather clock
Spoke.
Which would away?

Cool day, and no offence.
The breakfast things
Laid on a perfect table.
'Ragman eat your eggs.
It is a long way to go
And no reprieve.'

The Un-red Deer

The un-red deer
In the un-green forest

The antlers which do not appear
And are not like branches

The hounds which do not bay
With tails which do not swish

The heather beyond and the insignificant stumble
Of the horse not pulled up

By the rider who does not see all this
Nor hear nor smell it

Or does so but it does not matter
The horn sounds Gone away

Or, if it does not, is there hunter,
Hunted, or the broken tree

Swept by the wind from the channel?

The Deer-Park

In this bracken Diana
Of a surety is concealed.
Ah, huntress, the wonder to us
Is no longer the naked goddess
But the deer bounding
Of a surety from the brake.

Ah, little machines, like bounding
Shuttles above the bracken,
Like gnats on a fine evening,
Be pleased to represent for us
The universal machinery
Which else were intolerable.

We also are turning
In this fine evening
As parts of the vanquished world;
Your companionable fate
Is more now to the hunter
Than the girl's pretensions.

And the horn sounding at the death
Of the torn Actæon
Echoes for similar deaths
In identical forests
For in this machine world
No one can die lonely.

The hounds bear down upon
No individual sorrow
Or even identified pain
The certainty of reproduction
Is no longer the promise of life
But a co-terminous repetition.

It is possible that the musk ox
Descending the glacial valley
Enters the dying vision
Of the effete hunter, or the bell
Of the emerging church-tower marks
A point in the gathering mists.

Heroes

The heroism of the hunter
Is in his prey, is in his prey
The leaping animal
Always ahead of him.

The heroism of the fisher
Is in his catch, is in his catch
Which he examines
Like snot in his handkerchief.

The heroism of the aviator
Falling through space is the fall through space
A little moist jelly
Under a barrow.

Ellick Farm

The larks flew up like jack-in-the-boxes
From my moors, and the fields were edged with foxgloves.

The farm lay neatly within the hollow
The gables climbing, the barn beside the doorway.

If I had climbed into the loft I should have found a boy
Forty years back, among the bales of hay.

He would have known certainly all that I know
Seeing it in the muck-strewn cobbles below.

(Under the dark rim of the near wood
The tears gathered as under an eyelid.)

It would have surprised him to see a tall man
Who had travelled far, pretending to be him.

But that he should have been turning verses, half dumb
After half a lifetime, would least have surprised him.

Money

I was led into captivity by the bitch business
Not in love but in what seemed a physical necessity
And now I cannot even watch the spring
The itch for subsistence having become responsibility.

Money the she-devil comes to us under many veils
Tactful at first, calling herself beauty
Tear away this disguise, she proposes paternal solicitude
Assuming the dishonest face of duty.

Suddenly you are in bed with a screeching tear-sheet
This is money at last without her night-dress
Clutching you against her fallen udders and sharp bones
In an unscrupulous and deserved embrace.

Knole

The white hill-side is prickled with antlers
And the deer wade to me through the snow.
From John Donne's church the muffled and galoshed
Patiently to their holy dinners go.

And never do those antlered heads reflect
On the gentle flanks where in autumn they put their seed
Nor Christians on the word which, that very hour,
Their upturned faces or their hearts received.

But spring will bring the heavy doe to bed;
The fawn will wobble and soon after leap.
Those others will die at this or the next year's turn
And find the resurrection encased in sleep.

Cranmer

Cranmer was parson of this parish
And said Our Father beside barns
Where my grandfather worked without praying.

From the valley came the ring of metal
And the horses clopped down the track by the stream
As my mother saw them.

The Wiltshire voices floated up to him.
How should they not overcome his proud Latin
With We depart answering his *Nunc Dimittis*?

One evening he came over the hillock
To the edge of the church-yard already filled with bones
And saw in the smithy his own fire burning.

Tintagel

The clear water ripples between crags
And the Atlantic reaches our island
A clout on the outer headland.

A small band gathered God into this fastness
Singing and praying men; while others
Climbed up the perilous stairway shod in iron.

In every clearing a mad hermit
Draws his stinking rags about him and smoke rises
From thatches lately hurt by rape or pillage.

Cynadoc, Gennys, names as clear as water
Each hill enfolds, and the sheep
Pass numerous through the narrow gate.

At an International Conference

These are not words
In which a heart is expressed
You cannot catch in their rhythm
Which way the nerves twist.

This is not the lean orator
With palm touching the sky
It is not the beggar
Defining what is due.

This is not the actor
With tragic or comic mask
Nor the astringent Terpsichore
With whips for muscles.

This is the pot-bellied bankrupt
Naked upon the stage
With a porridge of news-talk
Obscuring his grimace.

Nude Studies

They are separate as to arms and legs
Though occasionally joined in one place
As to what identity that gives
You may question the opacity of the face.

Either man is made in the image of God
Or there is no such creature, only a cluster of cells.
Which of these improbabilities is the less
You cannot, by the study of nudity, tell.

The Art of Living

The child can grow
Only by being blind
He owes his greatness
To his fumbling.

The mind askew
From the appetite that drives him
The youth gives reasons
And has destinations.

The old man's waltzing nerves
Misdirect his hand
Aphasia, medicine, hope
Obscure his end.

Ide Hill

He sits with his gun across his knees
His fair wife beside him, with high cheek-bones
They are amorous without seeking to please
And fit to make their home among stones.

History does not remember enough to recount
Their ancestry, which is with ape and ant
Their manners are from the greenwood, the ground
Of their affections is patent as the sex of a plant.

In Honour of J. H. Fabre

My first trick was to clutch
At my mother and suck
Soon there was nothing to catch
But darkness and a lack.

My next trick was to know
Dividing the visible
Into shapes which now
Are no longer definable.

My third trick was to love
With the pretence of identity
Accepting without proof
The objects 'her' and 'me'.

My last trick was to believe
When I have the air
Of praying I at least
Join the mantis at its prayers.

Commuters

The slack faces
Of those in the train
Watch the bum-paper
In their sweaty hands.

Like folk in privies
They lean forward, each alone
Their visceral lives
Sagging within the skeleton.

If this is hope, they have it
The carriage will defecate
On the usual platform
They will find the amorous night.

Victoria Station

The man with nothing to say
May walk in a crowd
His assumed occasions
Will give him reason.

Those therefore whose tacit purposes
Do not allow of apology
Accept the plausible context
Of Victoria Station.

And my verse
Sidles like a child between categories
Instead of poetry I have
Only a location.

Family Fortunes

I.

I was born in Bristol, and it is possible
To live harshly in that city

Quiet voices possess it, but the boy
Torn from the womb, cowers

Under a ceiling of cloud. Tramcars
Crash by or enter the mind

A barred room bore him, the backyard
Smooth as a snake-skin, yielded nothing

In the fringes of the town parsley and honey-suckle
Drenched the hedges.

II.

My mother was born in West Kington
Where ford and bridge cross the river together

John Worlock farmed there, my grandfather
Within sight of the square church-tower

The rounded cart-horses shone like metal
My mother remembered their fine ribbons

She lies in the north now where the hills
Are pale green, and I

Whose hand never steadied a plough
Wish I had finished my long journey.

III.

South of the march parts my father
Lies also, and the fell town

That cradles him now sheltered also
His first unconsciousness

He walked from farm to farm with a kit of tools
From clock to clock, and at the end

Only they spoke to him, he
Having tuned his youth to their hammers.

IV.

I had two sisters, one I cannot speak of
For she died a child, and the sky was blue that day

The other lived to meet blindness
Groping upon the stairs, not admitting she could not see

Felled at last under a surgeon's hammer
Then left to rot, surgically

And I have a brother who, being alive
Does not need to be put in a poem.

Ightham Woods

The few syllables of a horse's scuffle at the edge of the road
Reach me in the green light of the beeches
Les seuls vrais plaisirs
Selon moy
Are those of one patch between the feet and the throat.
Possibly, but the beeches
And that half clop on the gravel
Indicate a world into which I can dissolve.

The Origin of Species

O let me die in a dark corner
For what is called the heart
Is only a tropism that any scorner
May name as he will, assigning whatever part

His own corruption suggests to this pain
Borne in my changing shape with changing lies

One aches towards God: he is called the saint
The lecher leans over a girl and sighs.

Whom I address from darkness: This mutation
Has failed, before I AM I hide my face.
Gather in without numbering this lost nation
And let a new creation succeed this race.

In Autumn

The sap is going out of my fingers
And the tune that my father used to drum
Comes readily to them.

Nothing that I could plead to young beauty
Could secure that my cold hand would be forgiven
Or the tears I cannot shed.

Well might Augustine pray that the ebb be not too fast
Holm-oak and myrtle and the treacherous bay-tree
Could not comfort him.

So turn me home towards God, and my last sunlight
Fall on no child of woman but on ash and chestnut
When the leaf falls.

At the Airport

Out of blue air
You descend like light
Child, not mine but me
Your heart in my mouth

But what seems similar
Across age, sex and size
Is no such matter
My look in your eyes
Brighter than in my own
My grief beside yours

Minute
And when I seem to burn
With a like flame I am
Cold ash beside you.

The Conversation of Age

Understanding is easiest between limbs
That run with the sap in them and have need
Of one another.

Longing may even appear in the eyes
And intelligence flicker for a moment in looks
Appealing for compassion.

Understanding is hardest between heads
Jigging away like machines in public loneliness
In the conversation of age.

St Gennys

In the granite church the wry priest
Handles the bread and the cup: and outside
Is a small windswept oak.

The mistletoe is cut down, but we creep
Naked as cats and dogs to this altar
Licking the blood upon the chancel steps.

On the Way Home

Like questing hounds
The lechers run through London
From all the alley-ways
Into all the thoroughfares

Until, shoulder to shoulder, they vanish
Into the main line stations
Or the Underground traps them.

A moment of promiscuity at nightfall
Their feet go homewards but their attentions
Are on the nape of a neck or the cut of a thigh
Almost any woman
As Schopenhauer noted
Being more interesting to them than those
Who made their beds that morning.

Maurras, Young and Old

1.

Est allé a Londres
Monsieur Maurras jeune
From a land of olives, grapes and almonds
His mind full of Greek.
Under the shadow of the British Museum
He reflected on the many and foolish
Discourses of the Athenians
And on the Elgin marbles.

The fog settled
Chokingly around the Latin head
Of the eloquent scholar
Quick like a ferret
He tore his way through
Scurrying past the red brick of Bloomsbury
To the mock antique portals.

The Latin light
Showed on the Mediterranean hills
A frugal culture of wine and oil.
Unobserved in their fog the British
toto divisos orbe
Propounded a mystery of steam
In France they corrected the menus
Writing for *biftec*: beefsteak.
Monsieur Maurras noted the linguistic symptoms
He noted, beyond the Drachenfels
The armies gathering.

II.

The light fell
Across the sand-dunes and the wide *étang*.
In their autochthonous boats
The fishermen put out
And came back to the linear village
Among the vineyards and the olive groves
Place de la République
Rue Zola
In which names the enemy celebrated his triumphs.

Twenty-five years:
Beyond the Drachenfels
The armies gathered again
Irruptio barbarorum.
The boats are moored on the *étang*
For Monsieur Maurras
The last harvest is gathered.

A Latin scorn
For all that is not indelibly Latin
A fortiori for the Teutonic captain
Passing him on the terrace of the Chemin de Paradis
Enemy and barbarian.
Inutile, Monsieur, de me saluer
His eyes looked out towards the middle sea
He heard not even that murmur
But an interior music.

Vienna

The heavy waters of the Danube
Flow eastward now from me away
The steppe creeps upon the city

I turn towards the distant seaboard:
    O island standing in the breakers
    God keep you from this grief of empires
    And may June see
    The dog-rose open in the hedge.

The Night Ferry

The turning and deceits of time
Do not allow to catch full face
Even the face of agony
But all is mixed and wrought to nought
In those evading corridors

Love is the light by which we see
The heart can hardly hold it still.

A Monument in Milan

Liberty is a great killer
All the *caduti*
Died in her name.
At every street corner
Someone crossed over in front of a machine-gun.
It is not only for the life that she promises
That liberty is loved.

A Duckling

I almost prayed for its departing
The tiny bird with sodden feathers
The Christian faith forbids such pity

The duckling weaker than her sisters
Crouching in straw within the hen-coop
Recedes from the immeasurable time.

So small a life with beady eye
Comfort cannot come at and none accompany
Entering among threshed ears the darkening shades.

In Kent

Although there may be treacherous men
Who in the churchyard swing their mattocks
Within they sing the *Nunc Dimittis*

And villagers who find that building
A place to go to of a Sunday
May accidentally be absolved

For on a hill, upon a gibbet...
And this is Saint Augustine's country.

Sparrows Seen from an Office

You should not bicker while the sparrows fall
In chasing pairs from underneath the eaves
And yet you should not let this enraged fool
Win what he will because you fear his grief.

About your table three or four who beg
Bully or trade because those are the passions
Strong enough in them to hide all other lack
Sent to corrupt your heart or try your patience.

If you are gentle, it is because you are weak
If bold, it is the courage of a clown
And your smart enemies and you both seek
Ratiocination without love or reason.

O fell like lust, birds of morality
O sparrows, sparrows, sparrows whom none regards
Where men inhabit, look in here and see
The fury and cupidity of the heart.

Fellfoot

They live in a solid cottage by the stream
And I know this of what is in their skins:
It grows to hope but does not seed to dreams.
They are the sort of country they live in.

Their limbs lie on these boards, heavy with sap.
The eyes they close are grey and green as stone.
They are not happier than trees perhaps;
When they are sad, then like the wind they moan.

The pot upon the hearth cooks simmering food:
Logs will not burn to ash in a whole day.
Their cankers are kept numb by a slow blood:
Slowly they twist, and turn from brown to grey.

Epitaph
These two in life did not discourage death,
But oh! it was like amber in their hearts;
Growing, at last it left no room for breath,
And they are hard and clear in all their parts.

On a Civil Servant

Here lies a civil servant. He was civil
To everyone, and servant to the devil.

In a Dark Wood

Now I am forty I must lick my bruises
What has been suffered cannot be repaired
I have chosen what whoever grows up chooses
A sickening garbage that could not be shared.

My errors have been written in my senses
The body is a record of the mind
My touch is crusted with my past defences
Because my wit was dull my eye grows blind.

There is no credit in a long defection
And defect and defection are the same
I have no person fit for resurrection
Destroy then rather my half-eaten frame

But that you will not do, for that were pardon
The bodies that you pardon you replace
And that you keep for those whom you will harden
To suffer in the hard rule of your Grace.

Christians on earth may have their bodies mended
By premonition of a heavenly state
But I, by grosser flesh from Grace defended
Can never see, never communicate.

La Biologie

The full creature dressed in her skin from top to toe
Is *La Biologie,* the famous beauty

The child, dancing and jumping to be or to possess this
The old, who scarcely knew when they passed this zenith

Claim separate minds in hope or in desperation
But blackness covers all, and the wind blows.

Moriturus

The carcase that awaits the undertaker
But will not give up its small voice lies
Hollow and grim upon the bed.

What stirs in it is hardly life but a morosity
Which when this skipped as a child was already under the lids
Rebellious and parting from the flesh.

What drunken fury in adolescence pretended
Merely to possess the flesh and drove onwards
The blind soul to issue in the lap of Venus?

The hope of fatherhood, watching the babe sucking
(Ah, he will grow, hurled headlong into the tomb!)
Gives way to a tenderness spilt into amnesia.

The last chat of corruption reasonable as a syllogism
The image of God is clear, his love wordless
Untie my ligaments, let my bones disperse.

Epictetus

I want to die creditably and with permission
Or I would long since have ended my days
The moon rises and the vast elms
Stand black at the edge of the haze.

Whether I live or die there is no I
Only the multifarious skelter of nature
Nothing except pride in this crowd
Marks out the rational (as they call him) creature.

The Body in Asia

Despite the mountains at my doorstep
This is a hollow, hollow life.
The mist blows clear and shows the snow
Among the dark green firs, but here
Upon the cold, scorched, dusty grass
The camels looped together raise
Their supercilious noses.
Upon the road the donkeys trot
And mule-teams with their muleteers pace.
The country lies before me like
A map I carry in my mind –
A wall built by the Hindu Kush
A plain that falls away to sea
I on the foothills here between
Sniffing the cold and dusty air.
Too long of longing makes me cold
The heart a tight and burning fistful

Hangs like a cold sun in my chest
A hollow kind of firmament.

I can imagine my exterior
The body, and the limbs that run off from it
But there is nothing in it I am sure
Except the ball of heart that weighs one side
Like the lead ballast in a celluloid duck.
And in my head a quarter-incher's brain
Looks out as best it can from my two eyes:
It can imagine how the country lies
To left and right, extensions of the limbs
But has no thoughts that I can understand.
Not only in this land I have felt it so
But on the Brahmaputra where
Bits of the jungle floated down
Black heaps upon the coloured river
When night fell and the sun
A red and geometric disk
Above its square reflection stood
For half a moment and then dipped:
I heard it sizzle in the water.
The flat and muddy banks, remote
Beyond the miles of plashing water
Diminished me
Till, smaller than the skin I stood in
I leaned against the rails and watched
The searchlights on the licking water.
The secret of diminishment
Is in this sad peninsula
Where the inflated body struts
Shouting its wants, but lacks conviction.
Conviction joins the muscles up
But here the body flaps and flutters
A flapping sail in a fitful wind.

In the Hills

Whereas I wander here among
Stone outcrops, rocks and roots
Below me tapers the peninsula
All India going to the sea.

Below, summer is a disease
Which seas surround whose glassy blue
Nothing can cool and nothing cure
But seize my heart

The jackal wandering in the woods
For I have speech and nothing said
The jackal sniffing in the plains
The vulture and the carrion crow

O jackal, howl about my bed.
O howl around my sleeping head.

On a Troopship

They are already made
Why should they go
Into boring society
Among the soldiery?
But I, whose imperfection
Is evident and admitted
Needing further assurance
Must year-long be pitted
Against fool and trooper
Practising my integrity
In awkward places,
Walking till I walk easily
Among uncomprehended faces
Extracting the root
Of the matter from the diverse engines
That in an oath, a gesture or a song
Inadequately approximate to the human norm.

Part II: Selected Translations

Foreword

IT IS NOT an impertinence to try to translate great masters. It is a tribute that one pays. Dryden, who had a right to speak, claimed only that 'some of the beauties of the author ... appear sometimes in the dim mirror which I hold before you'.

The question is, What sort of mirror? There are several kinds of translation. None of those in this volume is for people who want help in construing the sentences. But in a larger sense they are constructions, as any translation must be, a reading of the originals so that they make sense in our time. It will not do if one denatures the original, making out, for example, that Vergil was a smart-alec of the twentieth century. The aim must be to take what we can, and that can be no more than we can put into language that can be read. The argument is muddied by the critic's own reading of the original. A classical original is particularly susceptible of misconception, since people remember not only Vergil or Horace but the academy in which they were taught.

The method I adopted in translating Vergil is quite different from that used in my Catullus. There are two reasons for this. The first is the very different nature of the two texts. I am inclined to think that Landor was right in judging that a single poem of Catullus is worth the whole of the Eclogues. At any rate the language of Catullus is plainer and more direct, and that is what we now value, as Landor did, though in his day disapprobation of 'the Elizabethan style' was less common. It is proper to try to reproduce that plainness, as far as one can in the 'dim mirror' one holds. With Vergil the problem is different. There is a certain elaboration, very unfashionable in our time and perhaps of little use for contemporary literary purposes. There is also something which we ought to value. This is a deep movement of feeling, below the surface of our exacerbated daily life, and which has greater significance than any 'frankness' for those who want to understand the human brute. This is part of my excuse for translating Vergil on somewhat large lines. The other is that, for any poet, a translation serves a purpose and has a place in his own technical development. The exercise in plainness was what I wanted when I did the Catullus. The translation of Vergil was part of a movement away, as far as possible, from the merely personal concern, or from the presentation of our condition which has that appearance.

As to the versification, the publication of the Catullus has taught me that many critics will know what that should be. I have always found it a most difficult thing to know myself. Indeed I would say that there is no way of knowing except by doing it, and that all theory about the proper measures for a translation is out of place. There is no equivalent in English of Vergil's hexameter; it is not even the case that the regular couplets of Dryden represent it more exactly than a less regular measure. There should be a certain music, however faint. But it is an ineluctable law that a verse translation has to be done in the only verse that the translator, at the time of writing, can make; and that if he could not make verse before he will not suddenly become so gifted because he is faced with a classical text. Dryden wrote in the superb verse he was master of in his 'great climacteric'. For the Eclogues I wrote what I could manage at the age of fifty-three, after the last poem in *Metamorphoses* which in turn owed something to Charles d'Orléans. There is some development of the verse in the course of writing. The octosyllabic broke as I wrote, and although an *a priori* judge might object, a poet is not entitled to.

The translations here reproduced follow, more or less, a chronological order. The earliest are from Heine, an edition of whose *Meisterwerke in Vers und Prosa*, published in Holland in 1939 with an eye on the political relationships of the time, I carried in my pack when I went aboard the S.S. *Vollendam* at Liverpool early in 1943. This was the troopship on which the poem which closes Part 1 of this volume was written, and the book stayed with me in the camps in Bengal and the North-West Frontier Province in which I whiled out my fruitless stay. The Heine who was the Sword and the Flame of the German revolutionary struggles of the first half of the nineteenth century became the companion of the British Other Rank in his oppressive situation in the last decade of the British Raj. The translations were done for distraction, but they were the work of someone intent on sharpening his literary weapons, in case there should ever be a time and a place in which he could use them.

The odd bit of a French mediaeval song which follows is the survivor of a very small number of similar exercises undertaken, for pleasure and as part of my late and dilatory training as a writer, in the later forties but before I had resumed the writing of poetry. If I had been asked what I was after, I should have said *plainness,* not certain whether I meant in verse or in prose, and thinking more probably the latter. When I again took up, intermittently, the habit of writing verse of my own, my interest in translation became subdued. Yet the major outbreak represented by my *Catullus* began in a similar search for plainness, and with the conviction that one had not read the Latin properly until one could put it in language of one's own. By this time I had published *The London Zoo* and *Numbers*. The competition with Catullus – which even the best of writers must lose – certainly had its effect on the style of the succeeding volume, rather confusingly entitled *Metamorphoses* on account of some allusions to Ovid in the title poem. The Catullus translation began with a few specimens, the result of random browsings, and it was only at a later stage that it occurred to me – or rather to David Wright – that I might do the lot. I had had my eye on Catullus for years – as what poet would not who could make out even a little of the Latin? – but the actual translation was the work of a few months – months which were full enough already with business of a non-literary kind. It was a piece of education for the translator which, if my life as a writer had had any logic in it, would have taken place at the outset.

The next major work was with Vergil, and of that enough has already been said, except this: that with 'Palinurus' and 'The Descent' the use made of the original is so indirect that there might be some hesitation as to whether they belonged to this or to the earlier part of the volume. It is the balance of dependence which brought them here, while 'Eurydice', with its slighter allusion to Ovid, finds a place in Part 1. I have included in this part a frontal attack on Ovid, in the form of a version of the opening lines of Book I of the Metamorphoses. This is nearer than the Vergil to the spirit of the Catullus translations and was done between them and the Vergil.

The selection of my translations ends with some specimens of Horace, done with varying degrees of fidelity to the original. The version of the Carmen Saeculare comes near to being a new start from the old original, but it is closer to its text than the two extracts from the Aeneid, which are selected from a great number of lines, while this and still more the other Horatian translations attempt to find equivalents for at any rate most of the statements of the original. Horace is a hard nut to crack, and others before me have broken their teeth on him. But he does yield his nourishment and, in the measure that it is extracted, one becomes aware of a poet of great depth as well as polish – a poet invaluable in our time not least because of his lack of sympathy with our most current prejudices.

Heine

IN OCTOBER 1849

Gelegt hat sich der starke Wind

The wind's no longer blowing wild:
All is still as still can be.
Germania, God bless the child,
Is once more playing round the Christmas-tree.

We are content: the hearth-fire burns
And every higher wish deceives.
The swallow, that loves peace, returns
And builds once more beneath the eaves.

Peacefully sleep both wood and stream
With the soft moonlight over all.
Occasionally a shot rings out, a scream –
They've put a friend of yours against the wall.

Perhaps they found him with a gun,
A bit uncertain what to say.
(Not all have got the wit to run
As Horace did, and throw their arms away.)

Another bang! And this time, possibly,
It's crackers at a Goethe celebration.
It's nice to know that we are free
To enjoy at least this form of consolation.

And Liszt pops up again: how nice to see
This hero with us once again.
We thought him dead in Hungary
But, though a hero, he has not been slain.

Franz is alive, and in old age
Will tell his family, never bored
To hear of grandpa's martial rage
'And thus did my heroic sword.'

When I hear of Hungary
My heart swells till my skin's too small.

My hot blood rages like the sea;
The name sounds like a trumpet-call.

And when I hear about the wrong
We did them: how, against all odds
They fought, I hear once more the song
Formerly called the twilight of the gods.

Though the new song may be without
A hero, still it is the same:
The fighting and the final rout;
All that is altered is the name.

The same results from the same passion –
The flags fly bravely, but of course
The hero, in the usual fashion
At last's defeated by mere witless force.

This time the ox has made a pact
With the dumb bear, to get your blood.
But courage, Magyar: by this act
You suffer, but we too eat mud.

Plain wild beasts fought you till you broke.
It was a battle, and you lost;
But we have fallen beneath the yoke
Of wolves and swine, to our enduring cost.

Swine, wolves, and sneaking dogs: I can
Scarcely endure the victor's stink.
But quiet, poet: you're a man
But you are sick; rest now, and save your ink.

Es gibt zwei Sorten Ratten

There are two sorts of rat
The hungry and the fat.
The full and fat sort stay at home:
The hungry are inclined to roam.

They wander many thousand miles
And never stop between the whiles
They go right on and never stop
No sort of water holds them back.

They climb up all the mountains and
Swim any river in the land
And if some choke or die of drink
The others simply let them sink.

Rats, with their ill-bred perseverance
Present an impolite appearance:
They wear such proletarian hats
And look as sinister as rats.

These bolshie rats, it's very odd,
Have no idea at all of God:
They don't baptise their progeny
Their wives are common property.

The sensual and degraded beast
Does nothing else but drink and feast,
Preferring binges, on the whole
To care of his immortal soul.

Further, these wild, free-thinking rats
Do not fear hell, or even cats;
Having no wordly goods, or few
Want to share out the world anew.

Reader, these wandering rats, I fear,
Just now, are coming very near:
It frightens me to hear them squealing!
Really the beasts are most unfeeling!

We're lost! ten thousand of them wait
For us outside the city gate.
The mayor and fathers of the city
Are at a loss: a dreadful pity!

Abandon your important airs
Not peals of bells, or even prayers

Or special powers and regulations
Or bombs and guns will save the nations.

You won't convince rats they are free
By parliamentary oratory.
You don't catch rats with syllogisms
With soph- or any other isms.

The hungry belly, you will find
Is different from the well-fed mind:
It gloats for hours upon roast beef
But likes your arguments quite brief.

For fish and chips and cake and jelly
Satisfy the public belly
Better than a Mirabeau
Or any talker since Cicero.

Die Briten zeigten sich sehr rüde

The British took a certain pride,
Brutal perhaps, in regicide.
King Charles's sleep was somewhat light
In Whitehall on that fatal night.
Before his window sang the clown:
He heard the scaffold hammered down.

The French were scarcely more polite
For they – one cannot but reproach
Them for this dreadful oversight –
Forgot to send the royal coach
For Louis, when they took his head:
They sent a taxi round instead.

And then poor Marie Antoinette,
When her turn came, what did she get?
A farm cart and, as maid of honour,
A working chap to wait upon her.
The widow Capet scowled and bit
Her heavy Hapsburg underlip.

The French and British, unlike us,
Of course, are very barbarous.
Even as terrorists we show
Ourselves as kindly, dumb and slow,
We have, for the monarchic notion
A pious and absurd devotion.

And there will be a frightful stir
When we behead our Emperor.
We shall lay carpets for his feet
And, through the flagged, respectful street
In an expensive limousine
Conduct him to the guillotine.

Der Nachtwind durch die Luken pfeift

The night-wind whistles through the cracks
And blows about the attic:
The wretched couple in the bed
Look skinny and asthmatic.

One of these wretched people cries
'Oh, darling, put your arm
Around me, please, and kiss me too
For kissing keeps me warm.'

The other wretch replies: 'My dear
When I look in your eyes
I'm apt to think we have no cares –
Which isn't very wise.'

They kissed each other quite a lot:
They hugged each other, cried
And even laughed and sang and then
Apparently they died.

For when next day the P.A.C.
Official called, he said
(The panel doctor quite agreed)
That both of them were dead.

The doctor said he thought the cold
Combined, of course, with hunger
Sufficiently explained the fact
That they had lived no longer.

He added: 'When the frost sets in
The poor should put on woolly
Garments and eat good food: they don't
Appreciate that fully.'

Canto II: *Während die Kleine von Himmelslust*

Now while the seraphs sang their songs
Of love and heavenly peace
My baggage was inspected by
The customs and the police.

They turned my cases upside down;
They had to make quite sure
I hadn't any whiskey or
Forbidden literature.

Poor idiots, looking in my case,
You're hopelessly misled:
The contraband you're looking for
I carry in my head.

I have there many articles
Which, I am bound to state,
It is your job as patriots
To tax or confiscate.

I also carry other things
That you would think your pigeon –
The principles and blue-prints of
A curious new religion.

My head is full, I warn you,
Of the most disgraceful books,
And if I chose to take them out
You would not like their looks.

For, in the Devil's library
There are not books more beastly:
Some of them are as dangerous as
The works of J. B. Priestley.

A fellow-passenger remarked,
Watching the police with pride,
'These gentlemen ensured that we
Were fully unified.

'They give us outward unity
Under their manly grip;
Spiritual unity we get,
Of course, from censorship.

'Identity of thought we get
From that fine institution –
Which gives us an unshakeable,
If stupid, constitution.'

Por quoi me bat mes maris?
Anonymous, 12th–13th century

Why does he knock me about
    Until I moan?
I ain't said nothing 'gainst 'im
I ain't done nothing 'gainst 'im
– Just holding hands with Jim
    Us two alone.
Why does he knock me about
    Until I moan?

If he won't let me be
I'll do a thing, he'll see
He'll *have* to let me free
    Or I'll be goin'.
Why does he knock me about
    Until I moan?

Know what to do all right
To get my own back. Strite
I'll go to Jim one night
    Bare as a bone.
Why does he knock me about
    Until I moan?

Catullus

II.
Sparrow my Lesbia likes to play with,
The one she likes to hold in her lap,
To whom she gives her finger tip
To make him bite, as she likes, more sharply,
When, shining because of my desire,
She finds it a precious thing to play with
(I think, when her grave fire acquiesces
She finds it a solace for her pain).
If I could play with you just as she does
I'd have a way of lightening my cares.

III.
Time for mourning, Loves and Cupids
And any man of wit and love.
The sparrow's dead, my girl's own sparrow
That she loved more than her eyes:
For it was sweeter and knew her better
Than any girl might know her mother;
The bird would not move from her lap!
But hopping here and hopping there
Chirped for its mistress, no one else.
Now it goes to the darkened pathway
Out of which, they say, none comes back.
But curses on you, cursed darkness,
Orcus, you eat everything up.
You have taken my little sparrow away.
Oh, badly done! Oh, poor little bird!
It's all your doing, my poor girl's eyes
Are heavy and red with weeping now.

VIII.
You had better stop playing the fool, Catullus,
And accept that what you see is lost, is lost.
Once your days were shining
When you used to go wherever the girl led you,
She loved as none will ever be loved.

Then those many pleasant things were done
Which you wanted and the girl was willing to do;
Certainly then your days were shining.
She wants those things no more: you had better not want them,
Nor ask for what will not be given, nor live in pain.
Be patient, harden your mind.
Good-bye, girl. Already Catullus is hardened.
He does not seek you, and will not, since you are unwilling.
But you will suffer when you are asked for nothing at night.
It is the end. What life remains for you?
Who now will come to you? Who will think you pretty?
Whom will you now love? Whose will you say you are?
Whom will you kiss? And whose lips will you bite?
But you, Catullus, accept fate and be firm.

IX.
Veranius, of all my friends
The best of all of them,
And are you here again?
Back to your aged mother and
Your unanimous brothers?
Those messengers were welcome!
And shall I see you safe,
Talking over Iberia,
Its places, facts and peoples,
As your way is; draw your neck to me
And kiss your smiling mouth and eyes?
No one is luckier than I
At this moment, or happier.

XI.
Furius and Aurelius, friends of Catullus,
Whether he has a mind to go to India,
Where the eastern ocean beats upon the shore
Echoing far off,

Or to the Hyrcanians and the soft Arabians,
To the Scythians or the arrow-bearing Parthians,
Or to those plains which the sevenfold Nile
Dyes with its mud;

Whether he will climb across the High Alps
To view the memorials of great Caesar,
The Gallic Rhine, or the ultimate recesses
Of the barbarous Britons;

Ready although you are to do all these things
And indeed anything else that the fates direct,
The service I ask is only that you take a message,
Not a very nice one.

Tell my girl to enjoy herself with her lechers,
I hope she may manage three hundred at one time,
Not loving any properly, but leaving all of them
With ruptured arteries.

Tell her not to expect my love any more,
And that it is through her fault that it has fallen
Like a flower at the edge of a meadow
When the plough passes.

XXIII.
Furius, you have no slave, no money,
Not a bug, not a spider, and no fire;
You have, however, a father and a stepmother
Whose teeth could eat up flint-stones.
It is delightful, the life you lead with those two,
The old man and his mahogany wife.
No wonder; you all enjoy good health;
Your digestions are good; you fear nothing,
Not fire, or houses falling on your head,
Or thieving, or plots to poison you,
Or other occasions of danger.
But your bodies, drier than bones
Or anything drier you can think of,
Are made so by sun, cold and hunger.
Why should you not be well and contented?
You have no sweat, no saliva;
Your noses are absolutely free from snot.
To this purity one may add a more impressive one:
Your anus is cleaner than a saltcellar.

You don't shit ten times in a whole year
And then it is harder than beans or pebbles.
If you press it or rub it with your hands
You can't even dirty your fingers.
You should not scorn advantages like that, Furius,
Or reckon them to be small ones.
You should stop asking for a hundred sestertia,
Really you are well off enough already.

XXIX.
Who can see this, who can suffer this,
Except the shameless, the rapacious, the gambler –
Mamurra in possession of what before
The hairy Gaul had and the far-off Briton?
Depraved Romulus, can you see this and bear it?
Now he walks proud in his superfluity
Through everyone's beds like a leching pigeon
Or a handsome Adonis.
Depraved Romulus, can you see it and bear it?
It is because you are shameless, voracious, a gambler.
Was it for this, unique emperor,
That you went to the last island of the west?
Was it so that this worn-out codpiece Mamurra
Could squander twenty or thirty million?
What is that but the liberality of a pervert?
Has he spent little on lust and gluttony?
First he ran through his paternal estate,
The spoils of Pontus next, then those of Spain.
You should hear what is said in the Tagus gold fields.
Is this the man feared throughout Gaul and Britain?
Why do you keep such a man?
He is a general devourer of patrimonies.
Is it for this you and Pompey have thrown away everything?

XLI.
Ameana, the worn-out bitch,
Is asking for a whole ten thousand,
That girl with the flattened nose
That used to go with the Formian bankrupt.

Her family, or whoever looks after the girl,
Had better call in her friends and doctors:
The girl is mad, she has never enquired
What a mirror would have to say about her.

XLVI.
Already it is spring, the days are warmer;
The fury of the equinoctial sky
Gives way to gentle breezes, Zephyrus.
Catullus, now they leave the Phrygian plains,
Nicaea, with its rich and burning fields:
Now I can see the famous towns of Asia.
My mind is trembling at the thought of travel;
I am so eager that my feet feel strong.
I say good-bye to all the friendly cohort
Who came together from their far-off home
And wander back through individual ways.

XLVIII.
If I should be allowed to go as far as kissing
Your sweet eyes, Juventius,
I would go on kissing them three hundred thousand times;
Nor would it ever seem I had had enough,
Not if I harvested
Kisses as numerous as the ears of standing corn.

XLIX.
You are the best orator, Marcus Tullius,
There is or ever was among the Romans,
The best orator they ever will have.
Catullus tenders you his warmest thanks,
Catullus, who is the worst of all the poets
– As much the worst of all poets
As you are the best of all orators.

LX.
Did a lioness from the Libyan mountains
Or Scylla, barking out of the mouth of her womb,
Give birth to you? You are so hard and inhuman.
Your suppliant's voice crying in its last need
You treat with contempt, so very cruel is your heart.

LXIII.
Carried in a fast ship over profound seas,
Attis, eager and hurried, reached the Phrygian grove,
The goddess's dark places, crowned with woodland.
And there, exalted by amorous rage, his mind gone,
He cut off his testicles with a sharp flint.
She then, aware of her limbs without the man,
While the ground was still spotted with fresh blood
Quickly took in her snowy hands a tambourine
Such as serves your initiates, Cybele, instead of a trumpet
And, shaking the hollow calf-hide with delicate fingers,
Quivering, she began to sing to the troop this:
'Go together, votaresses, to the high groves of Cybele.
Go together, wandering herd of the lady of Dindymus.
Quick into exile, you looked for foreign places
And, following me and the rule I had adopted,
You bore with the salt tide and the violence of the high sea
And emasculated your bodies from too much hatred of Venus:
Delight the lady's mind with your errant haste.
Overcome your reluctance: together
Go to the Phrygian shrine of Cybele, to her groves
Where the voice of cymbals sounds, the tambourines rattle,
Where the Phrygian piper sings with the deep curved pipe,
Where Maenads wearing ivy throw back their heads,
Where they practice the sacred rites with sharp yells,
Where they flutter around the goddess's cohort:
It is there we must go with our rapid dances.'
As Attis, the counterfeit woman, sang this to her companions,
The choir howled suddenly with tumultuous tongues.
The tambourine bellows, the cymbals clash again;
The swift troop moves off to Ida with hurrying feet.
Crazy, panting, drifting, at her last gasp,
Attis with her tambourine leads them through the opaque groves

Like an unbroken heifer refusing the yoke:
The swift votaresses follow their swift-footed leader.
When they reach Cybele's shrine they are feeble and worn.
Sleep covers their eyes with a heavy blanket;
Their rabid madness subsides to a girlish quiet.
But when the golden sun with his streaming eyes
Purified the white sky, hard land, wild sea,
And drove away the shadows of night with his thundering horses,
Attis was aroused and Sleep went quickly from her
Back to the trembling arms of the goddess Pasithea.
Then from her girlish quiet, with no hurrying madness,
Attis remembered what she had done
And saw in her lucid mind what was missing and where she was.
Temptestuously she turned back to the shore.
There, looking at the open sea with tearful eyes,
With grief in her voice she addressed her native land:
'Land which begot me, land which brought me forth,
I am abject to abandon you like a runaway slave.
My feet have carried me to the groves of Ida
To be among snow in the cold lairs of wild beasts;
I shall visit their violent haunts.
Where, O my land, can I imagine you are?
My eye desires you and narrows as it turns towards you
In this short interval when my mind is unfrenzied.
Shall I be carried to the forests, from my far-off home?
Away from country, goods, friends, family?
From the Forum, palaestra, racecourse and gymnasium?
There is nothing for me but misery.
What shape is there that I have not had?
A woman now, I have been man, youth and boy;
I was athlete, the wrestler.
There were crowds round my door, my fans slept on the doorstep;
There were flowers all over the house
When I left my bed at sunrise.
Shall I be a waiting maid to the gods, the slave of Cybele?
I a Maenad, I a part of myself, I impotent?
Shall I live above the snow line on green Ida?
Shall I pass my life under the rocky peaks of Phrygia
Where the doe runs in the woods, where the boar mooches in the
  glade?
I regret now, now, what I have done, I repent of it, now!'

As these words hurried away from her pink lips,
Bringing a new message to the ears of the gods,
Cybele, letting her lions off the leash
And urging forward the beast on the left hand,
Said: 'Get on, be fierce, see that he's driven mad;
Make him insane enough to return to the forest;
He has had the impertinence to want to be out of my power.
Come on, lash around with your tail till you hurt yourself:
Make the whole neighbourhood ring with your bellowing roar.
Be fierce, shake the red mane on your muscular neck.'
Thus the threatening Cybele, and she wound the leash round her
   hand.
The beast stirs up his courage and rouses himself to fury.
He is off, he roars, he breaks up the undergrowth.
When he came to the wet sand on the whitening shore
He charged: Attis, mad, flew into the wild woods:
There, for the rest of her life, she lived as a slave.
Great Goddess, Goddess Cybele, Goddess lady of Dindymus,
May all your fury be far from my house.
Incite the others, go. Drive other men mad.

LXV.
Although I am exhausted by continual grief
And sorrow calls me away from the Muses, Hortalus;
Nor can what is in my mind be expressed in verse
So great is the trouble that shakes me:
For my brother has descended to Lethe,
The water is lapping his pale foot;
Under the coast of Rhoeteum the earth of Troy
Lies heavily on him, and he has gone from our sight.

I shall never again speak to you or hear you speaking,
Nor shall I ever, brother dearer than life,
See you again. But certainly I shall love you,
I shall always have you in mind in my poems
As among the branches and in heavy shadows
Daulias cries over the fate of Itylus.
Yet in the middle of this mourning, Hortalus, I send you
These translations from Battiades,
So that you will not think I have forgotten what you said,

Nor that it was as if you had spoken to the wind.
It is as if an apple sent to a girl by her lover
Fell out of her decorously covered bosom
When she, having put it in a fold of her gown and then forgotten it,
Is startled by the approach of her mother:
Then see how quickly it rolls down and away
And a self-conscious redness creeps over her regretful face.

LXVIII.

That, oppressed by fortune and a bitter event,
You should send me this note written in tears,
That, shipwrecked and ejected by the foaming waves,
You look to me to carry you on shore
When divine Venus refuses her sensual sleep
– For you lie alone in an empty bed
And have not the consolation of reading over the old poets
When your anxious mind keeps you awake –
I am glad of it, since you treat me as a friend
And ask me for provisions from Venus and the Muses:
In case you do not know my own troubles, Manlius,
And think I make a poor return for your hospitality,
I had better tell you I myself am under the waves of fortune
So that you do not look for happiness in this direction.
At the time when I first put on an adult toga
And my flowering years were at their agreeable spring
I played well enough: that goddess is not unknown to me
Who mixes a delightful bitterness with our cares:
But with my brother's death all preoccupations of that kind
Have left me. In sorrow, my brother, I accept your loss;
Dying, you have deprived me of my advantages.
With you all our house is buried;
With you all those joys have died
Which your love kept going while you were alive.
Since your death I have put of my mind
All such concerns and every kind of pleasure.
You write that I ought to be ashamed of myself staying at Verona
When all the young men about town
Are keeping themselves warm in the bed that used to be mine.
That, Manlius, is not a disgrace but a misfortune.
You will pardon me, therefore, if I do not, because I cannot,

Give you those gifts which grief has taken away.
For I haven't got many authors with me here.
That is because I live in Rome. That is where my house is,
My home; that is where I pass my life:
All I bring with me here is one box of books.
In these circumstances I hope you will not consider me ill-natured
Or think I am acting ungenerously
If I have not provided you with either of the things you ask for.
I would provide them unasked, if I had any.

LXXXVII.
No woman can say she was so much loved as you were,
Lesbia my darling, no one has loved as I have;
No trust was ever kept with such faith before
As, on my side, my love for you was kept.

XCIII.
It is indifferent to me whether I please you,
Caesar, or what is the colour of your hair.

CI.
Having come through many countries, over many seas,
I am here at last for these sad rites, my brother,
So that I may give you the gifts of death
And uselessly address your silent ashes:
Since fortune has carried you off,
Alas, my brother, wrongfully taken from me,
Now take these offerings which, by ancestral custom,
Are given as a sad gift to the shades;
They are wet with your brother's tears:
And then forever, brother, hail and farewell.

CV.
Old cock tries to climb the Piplean hill;
The Muses however chuck him out with forks.

From Book One of Ovid's Metamorphoses

My mind inclines me to discourse
Of bodies changed into new shapes.

Breathe on my enterprise, you gods
For these mutations were your work

And so, from the world's origin
Bring me down safely to our time.

Before the sea and land, before
The sky which covers everything

The whole of nature had one face.
This was called chaos, rough, confused,

A mixture of the seeds of things.
No Titan then lit up the world;

There was no Phoebe with her horns;
The earth did not hang in the air

Rocked by its weight, nor the long arms
Of Amphitrite hug the shores.

But where the land was, there was sea
And air as well, unstable land

Unstable sea and the air dark.
Then nothing stayed in its own shape

And everything got in the way.
So, in a single body, heat

Made war on cold, and wet on dry,
The soft on hard, and weightless things

Made war upon the things of weight.
A good and better nature put

An end to that and first cut off
Earth from the sky, and sea from earth

And liquid sky from thicker air.
Then having drawn the elements

From this blind mixture, the god put
Each of them in its proper place

And tied them up again in peace.
The fiery substance of the sky

Having no weight, came out on top.
Air, as the lightest after that

Spread itself neatly underneath.
Earth, with its heavy elements,

Piled itself quickly further down.
The water, flowing round about

Sank, and surrounded all the world.
The god, whoever he might be

Arranged things in this way, and then
Divided matter into parts.

And first the earth: he smoothed it out
And rolled it up into a sphere.

Then sea: he taught it how to spread
And blow itself up with the wind

And wash around the shores of earth.
He added springs and standing pools,

And rivers held by sloping banks
Which, in some places, lose themselves

And elsewhere flow away to sea;
Received in that free water they

Beat upon shores instead of banks.
He ordered plains to spread themselves

And told the valleys to go down,
The woods to dress themselves with leaves

And stony mountains to rise up.
The sky, divided into zones,

Two on the left, two on the right,
With a fifth, hotter, in between.

And underneath it is the same.
The middle country is so hot

Nothing can live there; the extremes
Are covered deep in snow; between

Two temperate regions, where he put
An equal part of hot and cold.

Above this spreads the air, which has
Less weight than water or the land

But more than fire. And here it is
The god sets up the mists and clouds

Thunder to frighten human minds
And winds that send the lightning out.

The maker of the world did not
Allow the winds themselves to blow

Across an undisputed air;
And even now, although they live

Each in his country, it is hard
To stop them tearing up the world

The brothers are so quarrelsome.
The East wind drew back to the dawn

Over the Persian mountain-tops;
The West wind hugged the evening star;

The howling north wind Scythia
Kept, and the seven stars by the pole;

The south wind wets the other side.
Above all this the god imposed

The liquid ether, free of weight
And also of impurities.

When he had sorted out the world
The stars, before that covered up,

Blazed suddenly across the sky.
And every region was filled up

With constellations and with gods.
The waters filled with shining fish;

The land had beasts; the sky had birds.
But earth still lacked an animal

Who had a more capacious mind
And could command the other beasts.

The man was born; either the god
Who made the world used his own seed

Or else the earth, so newly dropped
From ether, had some of its own

Or Japetus mixed with a stream
To make a model of the gods.

The other animals look down
But man is ordered to regard

The sky and, beyond that, the stars.
So earth, from having had no shape

Became the habitat of man.
The golden age was first, when none

Set up as champion of the right
Because there was no need of law.

There was no punishment, or fear
Or notices of penalties;

Nobody quailed before a judge;
All lived in trust and all were safe.

No pine was then cut down and launched
To take men into foreign parts

They were content to stay at home.
There were no cities with steep moats

Bugles and trumpets were unknown.
No swords, no helmets; no one fought

The time was passed in idleness.
There were no spades or ploughs, the earth

Gave freely all it had to give.
Men were content with what she gave

And took the fruit the trees prepared,
Wild strawberries or the acorns from

The spreading tree of Jupiter.
Spring was eternal, and the flowers

Sprang of themselves without a seed.
The field where none had worked soon gave

A yellow harvest of thick corn.
Rivers of nectar and of milk

Flowed past the honey-bearing trees.
When Saturn fell to Tartarus

And Jove began to rule, the world
Entered upon the silver age,

Worse than the gold, better than bronze.
Jupiter cut the ancient spring

And winter, summer, autumn came
To make the seasons of the year.

Then, for the first time, the air burned
And water was congealed in ice.

Men first sought shelter, and found caves,
Thick foliage, branches laced round bark.

Corn was first set in furrows and
The oxen first moaned at the plough.

The age of bronze came next, more cruel,
Combative but not criminal.

The iron age came last. All sorts
Of crimes irrupted on the world.

Shame, truth and trust were gone, instead
Came fraud and force, and perfidy,

And the desire of ownership.
The sailor raised his sail, although

He did not understand the winds.
From the high mountain-tops the barks

Plunged into seas they did not know.
The earth which had been common as

Sunlight and air, was parcelled out
And men were not content to reap

The harvests which her surface gave
But travelled in her entrails and

Dug what was hidden by the Styx,
The riches which would make them mad.

So iron and, worse than iron, gold
Came to the day, and so did war

Whose bloody hand employs them both.
Men live by stealing, and the host

Is safe no longer from his guest
Nor father from his son-in-law.

Brothers are without trust, and wives
And husbands wish each other dead.

Stepmothers mix the poison up;
Sons ask how old their fathers are.

The last immortal, Astraea,
Now leaves the impious, blood-stained earth.

To make the heavens unsafe as earth
The giants pile the mountains up

And try to get up to the stars.
Then the Almighty Father broke

Olympus with a thunderbolt.
Pelion was knocked off Ossa. Earth

      (*unfinished*)

In Allusion to Propertius, I, iii

When I opened the door she was asleep.
It is thus I imagine the scene, after Propertius.

The torches flickered all over the world
My legs staggered but I went to her bed

And let myself down gently beside her.
Her head was propped lightly upon her hands.

I passed one arm under her body
And with my free hand I arranged her hair

Not disturbing her sleep. She was Ariadne
Desolate upon the coast where Theseus had left her,

Andromeda, no longer chained to the rock,
In her first sleep. Or she was Io,

A milk-white heifer browsing upon her dreams,
I Argus, watching her with my hundred eyes.

I took kisses from her and drew my sword.
Then, through the open window the moon looked in:

It was the white rays opened her eyes.
I expected her to reproach me, and she did:

Why had I not come to her bed before?
I explained that I lived in the underworld

Among shadows. She had been in that forest.
Had we not met, she said, in that place?

Hand in hand we wandered among the tree-trunks
And came into the light at the edge of the forest.

Palinurus (Aeneid, V, 835ff)

Ho! Palinurus. Night came
Softly upon your dream.
The sailors lie, wherefore?
Slumped at the oars.
Your dream wakes still.
Not for long, while
Sleep hangs over the sea.
It is you she seeks.
Palinurus, innocent,
In quiet spent.
'Shall I entrust Aeneas to
This monster? Not so.
I have watched the fallacious air.'
Behold, god, the Lethean
Dew-laden branch is shaken
Over the sinking head.
You may call your comrades.
Palinure,
When Aeneas stirs.
'Naked and unknown,
Palinurus, your bones.'

The Descent (Aeneid, VI)

It follows my footsteps over these hills.

Some seek the seeds of flame
Hidden in the veins of flint.
Some crash through the undergrowth, point
To new rivers. But the same
Passions do not seize Aeneas.
He climbs where Apollo is.
And the secret parts
Of Sybil, in a dread cave,
Open, having the future.

Cut in the rock, lying huge,
A hundred mouths, you might say,

A hundred voices, Sybil responds.
To ask the Fates,
Time, it is time.
God.
Not one face or colour,
Her hair would not stay, nor colour. Panting,
Her breast like an earthquake,
Her heart swelling.
Not an ordinary voice. There is breathing
That is not her own, nearer to the god's.
'Do not stop praying, Trojan
Aeneas, must you stop? If you do
No gates can open.'

'Do not trust
Verses to the winds, but speak.
Leaves will not hold them.'
There was no prophecy. In such words,
Truth wrapt in darkness, that the utterance
Escaped my patience.
In such words, thus speaking:
'God's blood, Anchises'
Son, and a Trojan.
To descend, yes, through my entrance is easy.
Will you see the light again?
But if your mind is love, go down, cupid
Of the Stygian lakes, twice black Tartarus.
On a dark tree,
Golden, in leaf, the stem bending, a bough
This for Proserpina, a gift,
When it is torn, another and another
In its place, the same bough,
The same metal.
There lies your friend,
A corpse.'

Two doves flew.
They were my mother's birds, and therefore
Indicate.
Discoloured, in dark foliage,
As it were mistletoe,
Luminous on the oak.

Aeneas breaks it off
And carries it away under the roof of the Sybil
While on the shore the Teucrians
Paid to the last dust,
Misenus, your wishes.
The ground rumbled and the ridged
Woodlands dipped.
Through the unstable shadows
The dogs howled.
The goddess was approaching.
Then the vatic: 'Far
From everything, from this grove
Those who do not know love.'
The sword now out of the scabbard.
She entered herself, and Aeneas after.

Gods of the world of spirits, silent shades,
Chaos and Phlegethon lying in night,
Allow me to speak.
They went darkly, through night and shadows.
The whole kingdom was empty.
If there were moon's light, a wood,
A path in the undergrowth.
Night has taken the colours.
On the threshold, but inside,
Where Orcus begins,
Straw laid for Care,
With Sorrow upon her.
There are sick-beds enough. Age,
Fear, Evil Persuaders, Shortage.
They have terrible faces. Death,
Passing us ruthlessly. Sleep,
Also a brother, and the evil
Pleasures which exist only in the mind.
There were others. War
And one coifed with vipers.

A dark elm, huge, with dreams under every leaf.
Aeneas offers his sword to all comers.

I cannot however see the dead
Wailing by the water-side.
Why should they go over? A sordid
Old man, watching the girls.
Let them come to him. Charon,
Do not tip the boat in your excitement.
The dead are not lovers when
They pass your way.

I can hardly move now,
Aeneas, without your wishes.
There are several ghosts
I would wish to see.
And one especially, her hair
Plentiful where they have it,
Weeps from her head,
Too fragrant to be among the dead.
And beyond her,
One whose matted hair
Resembles Charon's.
Of him
Nothing is to be said, except
I came to seek him and
He does not exist.
The mist
Swirls up over Tal-y-maes.
He is gone with it.
An empty hill-side.
Fortune, if you are old.

A READING OF VERGIL'S ECLOGUES

Eclogue I

MELIBOEUS:
You, Tityrus, lean back below
The shadow of a spreading beech.
There are the trees your tuned notes reach.
But we must take our sacks and go
And leave these gentle fields and go.
We leave our homes but you lean back
Content to sing of what you lack.
Dear Amaryllis. The woods know.
TITYRUS:
How, Meliboeus, did this peace
Come to me? It was from a god
For he will always be a god.
I will hang up the softest fleece
For him. The gentlest blood will flow
Exact about his altar. So.
He lets me pipe my own release.
It is by his permission too
The heavy cattle wait on me.
MELIBOEUS:
I am amazed at what I see.
Elsewhere the people come and go
On all the wide fields restlessly.
Sick, I can hardly lead along
My herd of goats. Among
The hazels this one drops her twins.
They fell on flints, and that is that.
Oh, I was warned, dull wit. Heaven spoke
When I saw lightning rip the oak.
But, say, who is this god of yours?
TITYRUS:
I thought the city they call Rome
Was like another – our home
Town to which we drove our flock
On market days. I knew a puppy
Was like a dog, a kid was like

Her mother and I rather thought
A big town would be like a small.
And yet it is not so at all.
For Rome is not a city caught
By such comparisons. I see
A cedar in a shrubbery.
MELIBOEUS:
What took you there to Rome?
TITYRUS:
I went when I was called by liberty.
It did not happen till the day
The barber found my hair was grey
But it did happen. Not before
Amaryllis took me on
And showed the other one the door.
The other, Galatea, had
From me whatever I could earn.
With Galatea, every turn
Screwed me down tighter. Though I bred
Cattle enough, and rich cheeses
Were pressed in my dairy,
There was never any money.
MELIBOEUS:
I wondered, Amaryllis, why
You sadly let the apples hang
Untouched against the autumn sky.
Tityrus was away. So rang
Your name, Tityrus, and so sang
The fountains, and the orchards sighed.
TITYRUS:
What could I do? I could not leave
My slavery or find reprieve
From any other powerful god.
Our altars smoke twelve times a year
For that young man. I saw him here.
He spoke. And so the oxen trod
Once more across my fields. No fear.
MELIBOEUS:
You are an old man with good luck.
You stir around in your own muck
And cut yourself on your own flints.

Your lambs without disturbance suck
At the right teat. Your cattle munch
A cleanly hay.
Yes, some old men have all the luck.
Familiar rivers find their way
Past you. You watch the shadows play
And cool yourself. You hear the bees
Engaged upon your neighbour's trees
So willow blossom brings you sleep.
Your man sings at his pruning, you
May sit and hear the pigeons coo.
If there is any moan, or love
Expressing pain, it is a dove.
TITYRUS:
Have I not reason to be glad?
The deer may graze on cloud, the sea
Recede and let the fish go bad,
Frontiers may switch, the Parthians all
Drink at the Tigris if they will.
I'll not forget that young man's look.
MELIBOEUS:
We are not wethers for his crook
We must leave what we love and go
To warm ourselves in Scythian snow
Or quench our thirst in Africa,
Cut off from all the world, exile
Ourselves beyond the Britons' island.
For that young man will have it so.
And shall we ever see again
Our frontiers and our flat-roofed huts?
And see the few poor ears of grain
The alien soldier roughly cuts
From our dear fields? This is the gain
Of all these years of civil war.
This is what we have laboured for:
Now, Meliboeus, plant your vines
And sow your beans in ordered lines.
Come on, my flock, once fortunate,
You have not been so soothed of late
I shall not see you hang upon
My rocks. But you can still eat stone.

I shall sing no more songs, my goats
Hold no more clover in their throats.
TITYRUS:
You could have passed the night here, spent
A few green hours before you went
And shared my apples, chestnuts, cheese.
The cottage chimneys smoke, and please
The parting shepherd most of all.
See, from the mountains shadows fall.

Eclogue II

I do not think that anyone
Ever loved as Corydon
Alexis. Yet he understood
Enough to find his way to the woods,
Deep in which, out of the sun,
He regularly would make
To beeches and mountains
This complaint:
'Alexis, do you not care? Complain
I say but you drive me to death.
While I lack breath
The lizards look for shade.
The cattle cool themselves, made
Restless. Thestylis
Pounds for the reapers dishes
With thyme and garlic. While the sun burns
I seek for you by twists and turns.
There are, however loud I cry,
Only the grass-hoppers and I.
I should have had more sense and borne
With Amaryllis and her scorn
Or had Menalcas, though I knew
He was less beautiful than you.
But do not trust your beauty. White
Shoots end as withered twigs, the night
Falls on the hyacinth and rose.
Think, would you not do well to ask
How many fattened cattle bask

Under my trees, what honey flows
Out of my hives? Who, when it snows
Has butter still? Does not my voice
Conjure up luxuries at choice?
Nor am I so bad-looking when
Reflected in a pool or glass.
If Daphnis is the rival then
You might well think that I should pass.
Will you not lie upon my grass?
We have poor huts; you may come in.
I will cut you a switch.
You may drive your kids
Musically to their green meal
Or send arrows after the deer.
There are woods where we may sing
Like Pan, until he fears
A rival. Pan first found
Sweetness in pipes, he glued several
Together, he who cares for all.
Nor should you mind scorching
Your lip, as Amyntas did, with piping.
I have a pipe with seven stems
Damoetas gave me when he died.
Foolish Amyntas envied them.
I have two roebucks besides,
Found in a dangerous valley, they
Suck the ewe's udders twice a day.
Thestylis begs them. She shall
Have them if you turn away.
Come here you lovely boy, and all
The nymphs shall bring you basketsful
Of the chestnuts Amaryllis loved.
Add too the plum; honour that fruit.
And let the laurel have repute
Close to the myrtle. They have proved
Sweeter together. Corydon,
You know Alexis is not won
With presents, nor would presents make
Iollas give him up. No doubt
I was a lunatic to wish.
The storm has put my flower-beds out

And the pigs root among my fish.
Why run away? Alexis should
Know even gods may haunt the wood.
Pallas had founded cities, she
May well be true to them, but we
Have our obedience in the wood.
The lioness will track the wolf,
The wolf will track the goat, myself
Will have Alexis. Pleasure could
Have it no other way. Now look!
Over the plough circles the rook
And sees the sun go down in doubt
Which, ending, pulls the shadows out.
My love still burns. Ah Corydon,
What folly are you bent upon?
You leave the vine half-pruned, the dust
Gathers upon your withered lust.
There are toads under every stone.

Eclogue III

MENALCAS:
Whose flock is that, Damoetas?
Meliboeus's?
DAMOETAS:
                       No. Aegon's, or
It was, at any rate, before
He thought that I might manage as well.
MENALCAS:
Then hard luck on the sheep.
While Aegon feeds on air, and tries
To touch Neaera with his lies
You milk the sheep till they are sore.
DAMOETAS:
Be careful what you say. The goats
Looked at you with the eyes of stoats
While you did certain things. And yet
The nymphs laughed. Or do you forget?
MENALCAS:
You mean perhaps when Micon found
His vines all cut back to the ground?

DAMOETAS:
Or when you broke up Daphnis' bow
And pipe, because he liked them so
And they were not your gifts? Your spite
Exacerbated by delight?
MENALCAS:
I can recall another time
When I saw you in a sublime
Attempt at thievery. There was a bark
And someone running in the dark.
I called to Tityrus and knew
The rascal he would catch was you.
DAMOETAS:
I was just getting back my prize,
I won that goat. Damon admits
It yet he tries
To blame me for it, thinking this
Another competition he
Might win a bit more easily.
MENALCAS:
You sang against him? When did you
Play something we could recognise?
The only art you ever knew
Was whistling for a drink.
DAMOETAS:
You're too
Sure of yourself. Do you want to try
A competition presently?
If you win you shall have this cow.
She's a good milker. All right. Now,
What will you give me if I win?
MENALCAS:
From the flock, nothing. My father and
My stepmother are close at hand.
They count the flock three times a day.
Still, I will give you something. Say
This pair of patterned goblets, done
In silver by Alcimedon.
Do you see this engraving? Vine
And ivy closely intertwine.
Conon stands in the middle, or

Maybe some other astronomer.
He marked the stars out, showing how
To tell the time to reap and plough.
The cups, you see, are quite brand-new.
DAMOETAS:
I have two cups as well as you,
Made by Alcimedon likewise.
Acanthus creeps round the handles.
To one side
Is Orpheus with his following woods.
Why should I want your cups? I would
Rather have my cow.
MENALCAS:
You won't get off like that. Now
Here is someone who can judge,
Palaemon. He can take the pledges.
I'll show you what it's like to sing!
DAMOETAS:
So sing. If you have any choice
Favourites your voice
May sound them now. As referee
Whom you like. Palaemon, listen intently.
PALAEMON:
Now let us sit. The grass is soft
And every tree a miracle.
The time of year when all is well!
Begin, Damoetas, and as often
As he pauses, Menalcas,
You follow in, for that is as
The Muses like it: each in turn.
DAMOETAS:
And what does Galatea fear?
She drops her apples, then she goes.
MENALCAS:
But my Amyntas comes to prove
The value of the gift he throws.
DAMOETAS:
I have found presents for my love
A nest, and in the nest, a dove.

MENALCAS:
What could I do? My gift is this –
Ten golden apples, then ten more.
DAMOETAS:
I had her promises before
And may the gods remember me.
MENALCAS:
But what use will Amyntas be?
He leaves me to pursue the boar.
DAMOETAS:
Send Phyllis to me, Iollas,
Yet come yourself when you would see
A heifer slain.
MENALCAS:
      She cried 'Alas'
When I left her. 'O Iollas,
Good-bye, good-bye, you handsome boy.'
DAMOETAS:
No wind or hailstorm can annoy
Like Amaryllis in a rage.
MENALCAS:
Amyntas in his golden age
Is like a pleasant spring-time shower.
DAMOETAS:
Pollio has given my muse a shake:
Then feed a heifer for his sake.
MENALCAS:
Pollio himself has singing hours:
Then lead a bull to feed on flowers.
DAMOETAS:
He who loves Pollio will see
The honey dripping from the tree.
MENALCAS:
Bavius and Maevius sing like cats:
So plough with foxes and milk rats.
DAMOETAS:
You who pick flowers and strawberries,
Avoid the cold snake in the grass.
MENALCAS:
And sheep, be careful how you pass
The crumbling bank where the stream is.

DAMOETAS:
And turn the goats back, Tityrus,
The water here is dangerous.
MENALCAS:
Round up the sheep, before the heat
Dries all the milk up at the teat.
DAMOETAS:
My bull is weak and thin; the same
Love gnaws the master and the herd.
MENALCAS:
My weakness is not love. A game
Of magic strikes my young lambs dead.
DAMOETAS:
A riddle: in what land can eye
See no more than three feet of sky?
MENALCAS:
In what land flowers are crowned, and you
Show Phyllis something you can do.
PALAEMON:
I cannot judge who has sung best.
Not only both deserve to win
But anyone who has been in
The light or shade of love and pressed
Out verse should have a heifer. But
It is time the gates were shut.

Eclogue IV

Now higher matters entertain
This muse than shepherds and the plain:
Forests the consul would approve.
      The last age comes of all. Again
As Sybil prophesied, there move
The great chains of the centuries.
The Virgin is. And Saturn sees
His kingdom come like standing corn.
A new race now descends. And, please,
Lucina, when the boy is born,
Favour him. Let our iron give way
To all Apollo's gold that day.

    And you be consul, Pollio. Let
The months begin their process till
We lose the footsteps of ill will.
These are the fears we should forget.
He will have life from heaven, yet
Will mix with us and rule an earth
Made peaceful by his father's worth.
    But first for you, the child, foxgloves
And ivy demonstrate their loves.
Bean-blossom and acanthus laugh.
The goats come home uncalled, their milk
Serves itself for you. Lions eat chaff
And leave the herds untouched. The silk
Of your young cradle turns to flowers.
The serpent ends its poisonous hours.
The night-shade withers; in its place
Grow nutmegs, cinnamon and mace:
When you can read, the glory of
Your father, and the sombre race
Of patriarchs will guide your love
And all will ripen gradually –
The yellow corn, the blackberry.
Even the stubborn oak will prove
Its gentleness, by yielding honey.
Expect a few deceptions still.
There will be Argonauts to fleece
And how could there be perfect peace
With a new Troy, a new Achilles?
But, when you are firmly grown
You shall see trade and travel cease
And every country bear its own
Fruit and yet tillage be unknown,
The ox be loosened from the plough,
The sheep wear colours as they feed.
Run on the centuries which need
No spinning fates to tell them how.
    Now it is time for the new seed
To sprout and turn into a Jove.
The whole bent world bows down, and love
Enters the age that is to come.
Let it not find that I am dumb.

Whatever Orpheus sang in Thrace
Or Linus by Apollo's grace
Let me out-sing, to show that man
May now out-do Arcadian Pan.
      Time for you. Your smile
Eludes your patient mother who
For ten long months has carried you.
Time for you, for while
You dawdle, how can you be Lord
Of our expectant bed and board?

Eclogue V

MENALCAS:
Why not, Mopsus, since both of us
Have our abilities, sit down
Under the elms, and sound
You your pipe and I verses?
MOPSUS:
You are older than I, there is
No better rule of obedience.
Whether we sit in this pretence
Of shade, moved by the wind, or this
Cave across whose mouth the vine
Straggles, is for you to say.
MENALCAS:
Does anyone sing more finely
Than you? Amyntas perhaps may.
MOPSUS:
There is Apollo, the divine.
MENALCAS:
Begin, Mopsus, whatever way
You like. With love for Phyllis or
Praises for Alcon, or a whine
Against Codrus if that is more
To your taste. Tityrus minds the goats.
MOPSUS:
Something I wrote upon the bark
Of the green beeches, which I mark
With music. As Amyntas notes.

MENALCAS:
As willows to the pale olive,
Reeds to roses, I give
You preference before Amyntas.
We are in the cave. Let that pass.
MOPSUS:
The nymphs were weeping for your death,
Daphnis, hazels and rivers saw
Your mother hugging your last breath
And wriggling under the fates' paw.
No shepherd drove his flock that day
To the cool water, cattle lay
Parched at the edge and would not drink.
They bit no grass. The mountains think
Even the lions moaned that day.
Daphnis put the Armenian
Tigers to chariots and brought in
Bacchic dances, with leaves and ears
Of corn twisted round the harsh spears.
The vine lights up the tree, the grape
Lights up the vine, the dark shape
Of the bull dominates the herd;
Corn crowns the field, so your word
Impresses as the word of all.
The fates who took you were the fall
Of everything. As darnel grows
Instead of barley in the furrows,
For gentle violets and narcissus
There is the sharp thorn and the thistle.
Spread leaves upon the ground, bring shade,
Shepherds, where Daphnis is laid.
Heap up the mound and add a song:
'I, Daphnis, in the woods and long
Towards the stars was known. A fair herd,
Yes, but a fairer shepherd.'
MENALCAS:
Your song is such to me, divine
Poet, as sleep upon the grass
Or the shooting spring we pass
A summer day. You not alone
In music but in words surpass

All but your master. Though I own
You next to him, fortunate
Boy, I will imitate
You and raise Daphnis to the stars.
He loved me also. He was fate.
MOPSUS:
Now I lack nothing. He was far
The best shepherd and you are
A singer praised by Stimichon.
MENALCAS:
Now he has heaven at his feet
He wonders as he gazes on
The constellations in retreat.
And Daphnis now makes the woods glad,
The other countryside, Dryads,
Pan and the shepherds. So the deer
And flocks may wander without fear.
Daphnis loves easiness. The hills,
Where every tree still stands, may shout,
The groves, the very rocks, call out
'A god, a god, Menalcas.' Be
Kind to your servitors and we
Will raise four altars, of which two
For Phoebus, two, Daphnis, for you.
Two cups of frothing milk each year,
Two goblets of rich oil, and here
Upon the hearth, in winter-time,
Bacchus, and at the harvest-time,
Bacchus. It shall pour out. Then sing
Lyctian Aegon. Play for us
The satyr, Alphesiboeus.
These are the rites. Each year praying
The nymphs that they will bless our plough.
While boars run in the woods and fish
Swim in the rivers, then as now,
Bees sink their long tongues in the fresh
Thyme, and cicadas feed on dew
We will perform this rite for you.
Your name shall stand, the farmers say
Grace to you. Bind them as they pray.

MOPSUS:
That was a song which gave me more,
Menalcas, than I can repay.
Like quiet waves reaching the shore,
Like water among rocks, a breeze
Sibilant and quiet among trees.
MENALCAS:
I give you this frail pipe, which played
'Much loved Alexis' and 'Whose flock'.
MOPSUS:
Menalcas, take this crook I made
With my own hands for my own flock.
Antigenes shall not have it
Though once I would have thought him fit.

Eclogue VI

She sang Sicilian songs at first
And did not redden at the name.
Why should she? Muses are of the same
Mind as Apollo, that the worst
Poems are those with too much fat.
Spin thinly. Knowing what he was at
He took me by the ear and said
'Not kings and battles: sheep instead'
Now I (and, Varus, you will find
Plenty of poets to your mind
To sing of your heroic deeds)
Stick to this verse on country reeds.
But I will sing of you, and bind
Bearers to honour you, the grove
Shall sing of you and bring you love.
The name of Varus guarantees
That everything I write will please.
    You may sing, Muses. Chromis and
Mnasyllos saw Silenus lie
With swollen veins and outstretched hands,
His garland fallen on the floor
And his mouth open in a snore.
The empty pot will tell you why.

The boys approach and quickly tie
Him in his ivy. Drivelling head
That should have sung to them instead.
And Aegle paints it. May not she
The loveliest naiad, well feel free
With this old lump of lechery?
She plasters him with mulberry stains.
Silenus as he wakes complains
But says the boys shall have a song
And the girl something before long.
Then he begins. And see the fauns
Dance on the daisy-covered lawns.
The beasts in measure run, the oaks
Themselves bob to the tune. Phoebus
Is not more musical, or Orpheus,
Than the unbraced bellowing Silenus.
    For he sang how, through emptiness
The first beginnings of things pressed
The seeds of everything, and how
From this first fistful grew the world.
It was not then as it is now.
But the ground hardened, and the curled
Water receded to the sea
And soon all shapes wrenched themselves free.
The new sun is astonishing,
New clouds drop rain. The first time spring
Comes to the forests. Animals
Prowl on the new-cut mountain slopes
And are not recognised at all.
    Then he reports on Pyrrha's stones
And how the thief Prometheus
Was eaten in the Caucasus.
He adds how Hylas died, and all
The fountain echoed with the call;
Pasiphae was fortunate
Until she met her milk-white bull
And took him for a natural mate.
Proetus' daughters lowed like cows
But never tried to copulate
With beasts, although they feared the plough
And thought horns grew upon their brows.

Unhappy girl, upon the hills
You wander, while your lover fills
His belly up with hyacinths
And casts a licorous eye upon
Some heifer that he hopes to win.
'Then close the glades up, nymphs, he's gone
But you may tempt the animal
With grass or cattle to a stall.'
      He sings how Atalanta swerved
For apples from her virgin mark
And how those three young girls were served
Who found their limbs grow bitter bark.
And then he sings how Gallus wanders
Musing along poetic rivers
And all the choir rise to their feet;
To make the honour more complete,
Linus, a shepherd whose divine
Songs, locks and laurels intertwine,
Cries with an adulatory nod
'Here are the pipes of Hesiod.
He brought the ash-trees down the hills
With music and what you sing fills
Apollo's groves. It pleases him
Considerably to hear your hymn.'
      Shall I say also how he sang
Of Scylla, by whom the waters rang
With yelps about the Ithacan
Ships to the wreck of craft and man?
Or what he told of Tereus
Whose body changed its carriage as
He flew from Philomela's feast;
She circled upwards and, released
From human form, paused at her roof.
      So every song that Phoebus brooded
Over once and musically
Or that Eurotas told her reeds
Silenus sings, until the far
Echoes go up and wake the stars.
Vesper comes out, Olympus sees
The darkness come reluctantly.

Eclogue VII

MELIBOEUS:
Under an ilex Daphnis sat.
The wind spoke in it. Corydon
And Thyrsis drew their flocks to one
Place and accord. Corydon had
His goats distent with milk. Thyrsis
His sheep, and each their several ages
Green. Arcadians ready to sing
Both, and ready for answering.
To this place the great goat that led
My flock had wandered, and that is
How Daphnis saw me. 'Quickly' he said,
'Come over Meliboeus. Your kids
And goats are safe. If you can stay
Rest under this shade now. This way
Your steers will come to drink. The river here
Winds the reeds and your ear
Is entertained, listen, with bees.'
What could I do? I had no Phyllis
At home to look after my new lambs,
But the contest between Thyrsis
And Corydon, could hardly please
Less than my proper work. So these
Two started, with alternate tune.
One began, the other answered.
CORYDON:
You nymphs, my loves of Libethrus,
Either let me sing like Codrus
(Who, after all, is next to Phoebus)
Or if this cannot be, I hang
My pipe up here, where he sang.
THYRSIS:
Shepherd, with ivy decorate
Your post. Codrus will envy
Him or it may be
Praise more than reason. From this state
Protect him. If there are evil tongues,
Add foxgloves to the crown.

CORYDON:
To you, Delian, a boar's
Head, and the many-branched
Antlers of an old stag.
And if the fortune holds,
Diana, you shall stand
In marble, head to ankles.
THYRSIS:
Priapus, a pail of milk
And these cakes are all
We can offer yearly.
This garden is poor.
Be marble also. If fortune holds
You shall yet be golden.
CORYDON:
Nerine Galatea, come,
Sweeter than thyme, whiter than some
White swan, more delicate
Than ivy. When the bulls come late
From pasture, do you also come.
Certainly my bed waits.
THYRSIS:
May you indeed be free to hate
Me more than thistles, gorse or sea-weed
If this day does not bleed
More slowly away than the year.
Go home quietly, my steers.
CORYDON:
Moss at the springs, softer than sleep,
Grass, the arbutus's thin shade,
Protect if it may from the blaze
At midday, my worried sheep.
Summer is torrid, and the buds swell.
Laurels for Phoebus, but as long
As Phyllis loves hazels they
Chiefly shall make my song.
THYRSIS:
The ash is most beautiful
In the forest, and like the day
In gardens the pine, while the poplar
Is at home beside the river.

But if you came back Lycidas,
Easily you would surpass
Ash, pine, or any tree whatever.
MELIBOEUS:
I remember all this. Thyrsis
Had sung in vain. From that day on
The only singer was Corydon.

Eclogue VIII

The muse of Damon, shepherd, and
Of Alphesiboeus, I sing.
Did not the cattle leave grazing
To hear them, and the lynxes stand
Astonished, and the rivers stop flowing?

But you, whether you are now crossing
The rocks of Timavus, or coast
Hard by Illyris, what I most
Want is to sing your deeds. When may
I, when above all will be the day
I may make known your Sophoclean
Art? Meanwhile I sing –
A little ivy among your laurels.

The shadows of cool night had gone,
The dew was on the grass, when Damon
Sang, leaning upon his staff:
DAMON:
Be born, O morning star, before
The day in which I fill with tears.
Nysa sleeps with another. Hear
What you have chosen to ignore
You gods, now, in my dying hour.
    Begin, Arcadian flute, begin.
Mopsus has Nysa. The griffin covers
The mare. You may expect the deer
To drink with hounds without fear.
    Begin, Arcadian flute, begin.
Light torches, Mopsus, for your bride

And, bride-groom, throw the nuts. The star
Of evening brings her to your side.
    Begin, Arcadian flute, begin.
Gone to a worthy man, you are
Now one who hates my pipe and goats.
Well enough. Leave an old coat
And do not suppose the gods care.
    Begin, Arcadian flute, begin.
In our garden among the apples
I saw you first, the sap
Was new in me. I was twelve
Years old and you a child
Walking with my mother, I tell
Enough to reach the boughs. I saw
You and perished. What wild
Error bore me away?
    Begin, Arcadian flute, begin.
After that day
I knew what love is. The hard
Hills bore him, out beyond the far
Garamantes, Rhodope or Tmarus,
Not of the same race as us.
    Begin, Arcadian flute, begin.
Love taught a mother to find blood
From her own children on her hands.
Which of the two, Love or she, could
Be more heartless? Both in a cruel land.
    Begin, Arcadian flute, begin.
Now let wolves flee the sheep, the oaks
Bear golden apples, alders choke
With blossoms of narcissus, amber
Sweat from tamarisks, the croak
Of frogs pass for the nightingale
Or Tityrus for Orpheus,
Arion with his dolphins fail.
    Begin, Arcadian flute, begin.
Let all become the sea. Good-bye
To woods. I pitch from some high
Crag. And this with my last sigh.
    End now, Arcadian music. So.
That was Damon's song.

Alphesiboeus began before long:
ALPHESIBOEUS:
Bring water now, and round about
The sacred altars hand a fleece.
May I disturb my lover's peace
With burning herbs and magic shout.
    My songs, lead Daphnis from the town.
An incantation may bring down
The moon from heaven. And Ulysses
Was threatened by that song of Circe's.
Snakes split when a musician frowns.
    My songs, bring Daphnis home again.
I pull three threads around you, three
Of different colours, image, see
For heaven is a trinity.
    My songs, bring Daphnis from the town.
And, Amaryllis, tie three knots.
And call them lovers' knots, for what
Are three coloured knots if not that?
    My songs, bring Daphnis home again.
As this clay hardens and this wax
Grows soft in the same fire, Daphnis
The same. I scatter meal, and crackling
Laurel burn. Daphnis the same.
    My songs, bring Daphnis from the town.
So Daphnis shall feel love. As when
A heifer seeking for her bull
Sinks down at last to an amen
Beside a water-course, her full
Heart thinking no more of her home.
So may love hold him. And no pity.
    My songs, bring Daphnis home again.
These things he left me, which we
Valued together, bury
Them now. They are for earth. His debt.
    My songs, bring Daphnis from the town.
The herbs and poisons that you get
From Pontus, Moeris gave to me.
I have seen him in a dark cave
Of forest, become wolf, from graves
Call up dead spirits, seduce seed

Silently from another's field.
    My songs, bring Daphnis home again.
Bring out the ashes, throw them
Over your head into the stream.
And do not look. With them
I will approach Daphnis. He does not care
What god, what singing is in the air.
    My songs, bring Daphnis from the town.
Look, how the ash has broken into
Flame, with its own breath, while I
Hesitate at the door. The dog barks.
Shall I believe? Does this come dreamingly?
    My songs, bring Daphnis home again.

Eclogue IX

LYCIDAS:
Which way, Moeris, your foot? To town,
As the path goes?
MOERIS:
O Lycidas,
The day has come when our own
Is no longer so. Alas, with 'These
Are my acres. Go.' We
Evicted, in our grief, deliver
Up our goats to the newcomer.
LYCIDAS:
Certainly I had heard, these hills
Down to the water's edge, where beeches
Stand with their broken tops, had been
Saved by Menalcas, or his music.
MOERIS:
So it was said. But who fills
Himself with songs, when Mars
Bellows? They are
The eagle and the dove. Had not
An old raven from the oak told me what
Course to follow, neither I
Nor Menalcas, would be alive.

LYCIDAS:
Who falls into such crime? Alas!
And did we nearly lose the solace
Of your songs, Menalcas?
Who would have sung the nymphs? Whose hand
Would have scattered flowers here, and
Induced green shade at the spring?
And the day I found you going
To Amaryllis, with sweet songs,
Who would sing them? 'Along
This way I go, a short one, Tityrus,
Feed my goats till I come, it
Is a small matter, water them, and
Beware the butting horns, till I come.'
MOERIS:
Or these he sang to Varus. So:
'Varus, your name, if Mantus
Is spared, the singing swans shall bear
Past all suspicion of despair.'
LYCIDAS:
Your bees avoid the poisonous yew,
Your cows munch clover and are full.
If you have any song, so sing.
I am a poet too, the tall
Muses have given me songs, calling
Me as the shepherds do. I trust
Little to this. My songs are dust
To those of Varus or Cinna.
Among swans a goose-din.
MOERIS:
It is that I am searching
My mind for. It is no mean song.
'Come to me, Galatea. The cold waves
Are not the game for you. Here spring
Scatters her purple. To this cave
Come, there is shadow about it. In this place
The vines also embrace.
Leave therefore the cold shore.'
LYCIDAS:
What did I hear you sing, alone
Under the night? I half have the tune.

'Daphnis, why do the old stars hold
You? Have you not heard of this?
Caesar's? Dione's? It unfolds
Wonder on wonder. A kiss
Upon fields of corn, the vine
Ripening for subsequent time.
You put in the small shoot;
For your children the fruit.'
MOERIS:
Everything goes with age. I once
Had music in the setting sun.
It is forgotten now. Even the voice
Has gone. The wolf has passed this way.
There is no choice in a sad day.
But my songs eat Menalcas' heart.
LYCIDAS:
You give me your excuse. Now
The sea lies down below the ploughland,
There is no murmur to be heard.
We are half way. Bianor's tomb
Stands where the hedger clears the room.
Here let us sing. Or, if you will,
Sing as we cross the misty hill,
For rain may come. But if you sing
We shall have cheerful journeying.
I will take half your load; so come.
MOERIS:
Say no more, boy. I am not dumb
But we shall sing better when he comes.

Eclogue X

A last task, Arethusa. A few
Verses for Gallus, whom none refuse,
But such as, read by Lycoris, ...
But begin, Muse,
Fountain, slipping under the waves
To Sicily, unless you would have
Your waters salted by the crushing
Sea. Let us tell of Gallus

And his brow-knitting loves
While the goats nose the bushes.
Deaf, did you say? In the woods doves
Answer. In what groves,
What glades did you live, Naiads,
When Gallus died for love? In what sad
Walks? You were not on Parnassus,
No, nor upon Pindus.
No delay held you by
Aonian Aganippe.
For him the laurels wept. He lay
Groaning under a rock, the day
Parted over Maenalus, its crown
Darkened with tears.
The sheep
Stood around, sulking. Adonis also
Fed sheep beside a stream.
The shepherd comes, and the swineherds,
Slowly forward. A few words
From Menalcas, and from them.
'How is this love, to you?'
Apollo comes: 'Gallus, a true
Servant but a mad lover,
Your Lycoris is discovered
Among the snows, in camps. Another
Has her.' Sylvanus came, fennel
And lilies nodding upon his crown.
Pan god of Arcady, well
Able to ask: 'What way down
From this torment? Love does not care.
Never enough tears.
As soon satisfy
Grass with dew, bees
With clover or he -
goats with what they need.'
But sadly Gallus: 'Arcadians,
You will sing to your land,
As you are skilled, this matter.
I should be happy in another
Place, my bones rest, if you sang
My affections and the woods rang

With my notes as yours,
Shepherd or dresser of the mature
Vine. Surely either with Phyllis
Or Amyntas, or whoever is
The fury of the moment
(And is Amyntas dark? So are hyacinths.)
I should lie among the willows.
Phillis would pick me flowers, Amyntas
Choose a few songs. Lycoris!
Cool streams and soft meadows.
Enough to lie on. Here I
With you could consume time.
But now another affection, Mars,
Keeps me at the wars.
You too, far from home, far
From me, look at the Alps, hard
As they are, at snows and the cold
Rhine. Oh may the ice
Not cut your feet.
I will go free, and the reed
Accept my song. It is better
Certainly, in the woods, to devise
Marks of love on young trees,
Among wolves. They grow, and for her
My love will grow. Meanwhile to please
Myself with nymphs I will wander
Over Maenalus, or hunt
Wild boars, hounds
Circumventing the glades, though the cold
Bite like their teeth. What has been told
I see already, I am there
Among the rocks and forest, the air
Echoing with dogs. I imagine
Arrows from my Parthian engine.
As if this could do me good, or
That god mitigate sorrow!
Nothing we can do can change him, not if
We drank the Hebrus in mid-winter,
Suffered the Thracian snows, watery
And cold. Not if we,
Under Cancer, when the sun

Withers the bark of the elm, drove
Sheep for the Ethiopian
– We could not resist love.
He conquers, we give way.'
This is enough for one day.
Your poet sits, and his fingers
Weave baskets of the slender
Hibiscus. And for Gallus
These songs shall be enough.
Gallus, for whom my love
Grows hourly, as in spring
New shoots in everything.
Let us go now, the shade
Brings danger to singers.
The juniper is afraid.
Without the sun nothing
Will ripen. Go home,
Full goats. Hesperus comes.

Horace

Carmen Saeculare

O sun, and moonlight shining in the woods,
The best things in heaven, always to be worshipped
As long as they give us exactly what we want

Now, at this season when selected girls
And the boys who are about to venture upon them,
Though still in bud, sing what will please London,

As you bring out one day and conceal another
Shine on the arms and legs and make them brown.
May all you see be greater than we are.

The time will come to open thighs in child-birth.
Gently, supervising god, look after the mothers.
Bringing to light is the true meaning of genitals.

Could you bring up these children without laws?
The statute-book is crowded, what wonder therefore
If all that interests them is an obscure kindness?

A hundred and ten years it may easily be
Before songs and games which come as speedily
As these three days, ah, and delicious nights.

You have sung truthfully enough, O fates.
Once it was ordained that everything should be stable
And will be again, but not now, or for ever.

Rich in apples, yes, and seething with cattle,
The succulent earth is dressed in barley whiskers.
And grow plump, embryo, from the natural gifts.

The sun will shine, as long as the boys are suppliant,
That will keep sickness away; and you girls,
Listen, for the moon will hear you if you do.

If you made London, as before it Engelland,
The Jutes coming over in ships, but only to be Romans,
Part of that remnant to join this one

The ways that have led here are multifarious,
Even Brutus from Troy, our ancestors believed,
But whatever they left they found better here.

You cannot credit the wish, that the young should be teachable
And old age quiet. Yet it is these wishes
Spring from the earth at last, when the country flowers.

Might you not even remember the old worship?
I could name ancestors, it is not done any more.
It remains true that, before you are king, you must win.

We have been through it all, victory on land and sea,
These things were necessary for your assurance.
The King of France. Once there was even India.

Can you remember the expression 'Honour'?
There was, at one time, even Modesty.
Nothing is so dead it does not come back.

There is God. There are no Muses without him.
He it is who raises the drug-laden limbs
Which were too heavy until he stood at Saint Martin's.

It is he who holds London from Wapping to Richmond,
May he hold it a little longer, Saint George's flag
Flap strenuously in the wind from the west country.

Have you heard the phrase: 'the only ruler of princes'?
Along the Thames, in the Tower, there is the crown.
I only wish God may hear my children's prayers.

He bends now over Trafalgar Square.
If there should be a whisper he would hear it.
Are not these drifting figures the chorus?

Iam satis terris nivis atque dirae (I, ii)

Already enough snow, hail, thunder and lightning
Our Father has sent us, bloody-handed.
He has thrown down the Capitoline buildings
        And terrified the city,

Terrified the inhabitants, who fear the return
Of the age of Pyrrha, a time of floods and marvels
When Proteus led his monsters up to the hill-tops
        Although they belonged to the sea,

And the whole genus of fishes found its way to the elm-tops
Which were more accustomed to entertaining pigeons
And the tender-eyed deer found themselves permanently swimming
        On a limitless ocean.

We saw the yellow ochre of the Tiber
Turned back violently at the mouth by the Etruscan sea,
Flooding over Numa's monument, wrecking also
        The temple of Vesta

When, for the sake of the querulous Ilia
In vengeance he threw himself, spreading
Far over the left bank, in defiance of Jove;
        The stream is uxorious.

He heard that the Romans had been sharpening their knives
To cut up one another – it would have been better to cut up the
   Persians –
Heard also that children had become scarce,
        Their parents being vicious.

Which of the gods is it best for the people to call upon
When the empire is falling? What prayers are best for the Vestals
To use in a time like this, though their goddess
        Pays little attention?

Jupiter has to give someone the task of expiation.
Come, as we pray, your muscular shoulders shining
In a cloak of cloud, you perhaps were the best,
        Far-seeing Apollo,

Or, if you prefer, send us the smiling Venus,
With every delight as usual flying about her
Or, if the neglected race of your progeny
        Deserves that attention,

Father of Romulus, you have seen enough of war,
It has gone on too long, forget the sort of spectacle
You are most at home with, the Moorish foot-soldier
        Desperate against his enemy.

Or, changing your shape, as you come among us on earth,
Son of Maia – she will be kind – assume the appearance
Of this man still in his prime, and well suited to be
        The avenger of Caesar.

Go back late to heaven, and meanwhile
Be among your people, the Quirinals
And I pray only that no fault of theirs may
        Drive you away.

Here rather may you enjoy the triumphs you love,
A prince and our benefactor;
Do not leave even the Medes unpunished
        While you lead us, Caesar.

Tu ne quaesieris, scire nefas, quem mihi, quem tibi (I, xi)

You do not ask – useless to ask, Leuconoë –
What end the gods will give, to me, to you.
Consult no augurers. Suffer what comes,
Whether some winters still, or this one only
Which now wears out the sea under the cliffs.
Think, take your wine. You are better off with sleep
And no long hopes. For, while we speak, age falls.
Collect your day, and have it. The next, you may not.

Quid dedicatum poscit Apollinem (I, xxxi)

When he makes his petition to Apollo
What does the poet ask for? What, as he pours
New liquor out of the cup? Not rich
Estates in Sardinia, heavy with wheat,

Nor in burning Calabria, with herds
Of cattle. Not ivory and gold from
India. Not even the fields whose edges
The Liris nibbles with her quiet waters.

Those to whom fortune allows it can trim
The vine with Calenian pruning-knives, so that
The well-to-do business man can drain
Wine from golden cups, on the strength of the Syrian trade.

He is dear to the gods themselves, since he sails
In the Atlantic three or four times a year
Without disaster. I feed on olives,
Chicory is my meat, I eat mallow.

Allow me to be content with what I've got,
Latona's son and, I pray, to pass my age
Well and sensible, without disgrace
And not, I beg you, without the Muse.

Rectius vives, Licini, neque altum (II, x)

You live more suitably, Licinius, if you're not
Always pressing out to sea or, on the other hand,
In your anxiety to avoid storms, always
Skirting the dangerous rocks.

Whoever is able to choose the half-way house
Is safe, on the one hand, from living in a slum
And with equal discretion avoids the residence
That his neighbours will envy.

It is most often the tall pine that is shaken
By the wind and it is the high towers which go down
With the heaviest crash, while lightning strikes the highest
Mountains for preference.

Hopeful in adversity, fearful when in luck,
The heart is always ready for the opposite
Of what happens. Jupiter brings in the shapeless
Winters but he also

Takes them away. If things are bad now, and have been,
They will not always be so. Sometimes Apollo
Rouses the silent Muse with his lyre; he is not
Always stretching his bow.

When times are difficult put on the appearance
Of courage; but if the wind is too favourable,
As it can be, the judicious thing
Is to trim your sails.

Iam pauca aratro iugera regiae (II, xv)

There will be nothing soon for the plough
But huge bulks everywhere. On all sides
    Wider than lakes, the city
    Lamp-standards drive out the elms,

Planes, beeches. Once it was fertile here.
Edges of violets circumscribed
    The grove; there was everywhere something for the
    Nostrils, but now there is nothing.

Where there were once forests a region of
Concrete. Until quite recently
    There were meadows at Westminster.
    The salmon leaped where Raleigh was beheaded.

Once there was only nature for ornament.
Then there was ornament and art flourished;

Now there is only the South Bank
And, of course, the Arts Council.

It was not laws but a less abstract
Technology made the turf spring.
    The churches in those days, you may
    Remember, were built of stone.

Eheu fugaces, Postume, Postume (II, xiv)

The years go by, the years go by you, nameless,
I cannot help it nor does virtue help.
    Wrinkles are there, old age is at your elbow,
    Death on the way, it is indomitable.

Not if you choose, as you will choose, to doctor
Yourself with hope, will you weep out your pain.
    The underworld is waiting. There are monsters
    Such as distended you before you died.

The subterranean flood is there for everyone who has taken food and drink on earth.
    A light skiff will put out, you will be on it –
    And, win the pools, you still will go aboard.

The blood dried on you and you came home safely
– Useless. You blew out an Atlantic storm.
    – No need to fear the wind, it can do no harm.
    It brings you where you will be brought at last.

The dark, the black and, in the blackness, water,
A winding stream, it will not matter to you.
    The fifty murderesses are there, the toiler,
    Exhaustion beyond hope, condemned to dreams.

Your house, your wife, and the familiar earth,
All will recede, and of the trees you prune
    Only the cypress follow you, ill-omened.
    You were here briefly, you are here no more.

The heir you leave is better than yourself,
What you kept closest he will throw away.
  Your books are on the pavement, and his laughter
  Sounding like broken glass through all the rooms.

LIBRARY OF DAVIDSON COLLEGE